Praise for *I*

"There is a well-known saying among writers, 'Happiness writes white.' But in reminiscences of a joyful childhood, perfect nachos, and blissful summer days, *Border Town Chica* sets happiness to the page in ink."

— Rena Priest, *Washington State Poet Laureate*

"A thoroughly engaging and enjoyable tapestry of personal experiences and insights, *Border Town Chica* delivers universal affirmations of life that manage to both entertain and inform. From moments of simple beauty, complications, lessons, joy and pain, the conveyance here is clear—pay attention and be both gracious and grateful. The world would be a far better place should more of us choose to follow the author's example."

— D. W. Ulsterman, bestselling author of the San Juan Islands Mysteries

"Patricia, I enjoyed reading your book. It reminded me so much of my own childhood growing up in a Sicilian household. I could relate to the strong family unit, the huge amount of respect for parents, and the colorful cultural background. Your stories are delightful recollections . . . from the delicious cuisine and exuberant fiestas, to the tale of the evil eye. *You don't play around with the evil eye!* And then of course, the Christmas tamales which made me hungry. This book is an opportunity to appreciate and celebrate life's everyday moments with love and joy."

— Bob Badami, Hollywood Film Music Supervisor

"*Border Town Chica* is a charming collection of childhood remembrances written with the warmth of a steaming handmade tortilla taken fresh out of the pan. Patricia's mouth-watering descriptions of her favorite foods served up with a heap of family love and care will restore your faith in humanity *and* your appetite! Delightful vignettes to savor for your bedtime read. Highly recommended!"

– Elizabeth B Jenkins,
International Bestselling Author

"Poised, polished remembrances."

– Kirkus Reviews

For a full review of the previous/first edition from Kirkus Reviews, please visit:
https://www.kirkusreviews.com/book-reviews/patricia-alarcon-missler/pink-elephants-and-chocolate-eclairs/.

BORDER TOWN
CHICA

A Memoir

To my palo,
Ray & Carol ♡
patricia

patricia alarcón missler

PATRICIA ALARCÓN MISSLER

CORNER
HOUSE
PUBLISHING

Library of Congress Control Number: 2013915990

ISBN: 979-8-9900621-0-8 (Paperback)
ISBN: 979-8-9900621-1-5 (eBook)

All photographs, copyright © 2013 by Patricia Missler
Layout and design by Book House Publishing
Book jacket © 2024 by Book House Publishing
and Bob Paltrow Design
Photograph of author by Robert J. Jaffe

Printed in the USA by Village Books

CORNER HOUSE PUBLISHING
books@cornerhousepublishing.com

*For my loving mother, Rosario,
whose presence graced my life.*

Contents

Author's Note

AFTER ALMOST FOUR DECADES OF CALLING the island of Hawaii home, it was time for a fresh perspective. My husband and I were drawn to the natural beauty of the Pacific Northwest. We moved to Bellingham, Washington in 2021.

With such a dramatic move comes the opportunity for reinvention, enabling me to redefine and expand the vision of my continued creative journey. Engaging with a new literary and art community has become a large part of who I am.

This expanded awareness has given birth to a revised edition of my original book, *Pink Elephants and Chocolate Éclairs: Memoir of a Border Town Chica*, published in 2014. It now comes to you, a decade later, with a makeover.

My revised edition is aptly named *Border Town Chica, A Memoir.* The title change is more reflective of the stories within. The book cover has been redesigned and a bonus short story has been included.

I hope you enjoy *Border Town Chica, A Memoir.*

Preface

THE DECISION TO WRITE THIS BOOK of stories about my life came to me one morning while driving to work. The morning drive was peaceful. The cool breeze blowing through the car windows carried a hint of jasmine-like scent from the surrounding coffee trees that were in full bloom. It was a moment of grace. As I lingered in that feeling, my heart felt gratitude for the wonderful life my parents had struggled to give me.

I began in earnest to reflect upon the early years of my life growing up in Brownsville, a small town in South Texas that borders Mexico along the Rio Grande. These memories highlighted the infinite softness and giving of my mother, the stoic demeanor of my father, the dignity of my grandmother, the playfulness of my aunt, and the deep connection with my siblings. There was plenty of laughter in the process of writing some of these stories, and there were also tears.

By remembering how colorful my past was, I was able to embrace who I am today with more love, understanding, and pride. I acknowledge and thank my family for the treasured traditions that they shared with me, making me who I am today.

This journey has been a pivotal experience for me. And I've emerged a changed person . . . amazed at how rich my past was and how vital an ingredient it is in my present and my future.

For my parents,
Alfredo Guillermo Alarcón Luna
and María del Rosario Medina de Alarcón.
While on their honeymoon in Mexico City on December 9, 1940,
a street photographer took a photo of my parents.

Vannie Tilden

I SUPPOSE IT WAS NOT ONLY THE luscious pastries at the popular local bakery, Vannie Tilden, that I loved so much. It wasn't just the cream horns, the chocolate éclairs, the cream puffs, or the delicate milk chocolate brownies that captivated my taste buds. It was the whole adventure—the idea of going in to town for a special treat on a Saturday morning. The driving there. The getting there. The looking at the stark white building that was a cross between Art Deco and Modern. The front of the building had enormous glass windows that enhanced the view of the pastry cases as soon as you drove up and parked your car outside the front door. I felt like I was in some wonderful astral plane, and I didn't even know what an astral plane was back then (not that I know now either . . .).

Anyway, there I was, a little kid in my favorite brown corduroy pants, white T-shirt, and special red cowboy boots hopping out of the car with my long golden-brown braids dangling next to my ears. Jumping out after me was my older sister, Irene (or, as we called her, Nene), who wore a dainty floral dress that had a ruffle around the neck and black patent-leather Mary Janes with white ruffled socks. We were quite a pair. Frick and Frack, Tom and Jerry, Lucy and Ethel? I don't know exactly who we resembled, but we were having fun.

HERE I AM AT AGE SIX, SPORTING MY LONG HAIR, CORDUROY PANTS, AND FAVORITE COWBOY BOOTS.

Then there was my father who always dressed to impress, not that he meant to, of course. Kind of like a male version of Jackie O. Like my father, Jackie could do no wrong with her style in her black slacks, classic white shirt, black designer flats, signature scarf, and the oversized sunglasses insuring her a bit of anonymity and glamour. Suffice it to say my father had that same Jackie O. DNA; he always looked sharp, classic, and debonair, no matter what he wore. I think all of us girls, to a greater or lesser degree, inherited that trait from my father. We were all sharp dressers, too, not that we were trying either. Definitely the trendsetters in school, thanks to my mother's expert tailoring that insured us countless fashion triumphs.

My sister and I timidly entered that unfamiliar world with our well-dressed *caballero*, our tall gentleman with the tailored pleated pants, long-sleeved white shirt, skinny black tie, and wool felt Stetson hat, each of us grabbing on to one of his big tanned hands. I am sure he had a million better things to do with his time and hard-earned money, yet every so often on a sleepy Saturday morning, he would take the time for this excursion into the fancy bakery world of Vannie Tilden, into a world he knew was different from our own.

Although I didn't understand the looks at the time, the women who worked at the pastry counter must have wondered about this handsome man. Lisa, the prettier of the two women, would always offer a sample of the baker's latest creation. My dad would swiftly shake his head with a firm "no, thank you" and simply begin asking us what we wanted to take home. Looking back at those times, I realize that my father was still relatively young and attractive. He appeared to be oblivious of the counter girls looking at him with their warm, brown, seductive eyes. That was a really good thing for us because my parents remained happily married their whole lives until my father passed away in his seventies.

As for the flavor of my childhood besides going to wonderful bakeries and other assorted eateries, I grew up in South Texas in the 1950s. Ours was a very friendly mixed neighborhood with Mexican American and Anglo families. I suppose that was the beginning of a modest middle-class neighborhood in Brownsville. Our elementary school, Ebony Heights, was one block to the east of our house, and we could easily run home for lunch if we wanted. It was a time when you didn't have to worry about your kids walking home without adult supervision. I guess we were lucky that way. Life was so uncomplicated. It continued that way pretty much up to our college days, and then things began to turn. The late sixties with Vietnam, protests, . . . but this story isn't about those days.

Venturing out to this type of pastry shop was unique because it was not the sort of bakery a Mexican immigrant or first-generation Mexican American would normally enter, let alone buy pastry to go. Cream puffs, éclairs, cream horns, Danish, pecan rolls—what the heck were those? They just weren't a part of our cultural heritage or vocabulary. At least not yet. That was what you got at Vannie Tilden.

There was, however, a very traditional Mexican *panadería* (bakery) that we also frequented, cleverly named First Street Bakery (located on First Street). It was in the old part of downtown Brownsville on the other side of the railroad tracks. A Mexican panadería was not at all like the VT experience. It was an entirely different world.

Strategically placing our hands and noses on the glass fronts of the display cases at Vannie Tilden, Nene and I proceeded to gingerly pick out our own personal favorites, all the while keeping in mind our older siblings and our mother, of course. We always tried to pick the most beautiful piece in the entire display case for Mami. We instinctively knew she had few moments in her life filled with beauty just for beauty's sake.

So my sister and I, and I suppose my father in his own way, wanted to give her a moment to relish perfection, even if it was just in the flawless creamy swirl at the end of a cream horn or the silver candied beads on a hand-embellished vanilla cupcake with light-pink buttercream icing. Whatever we picked out for her had to be the best, no matter the cost. My father would often let out a deep sigh at the pricey pieces we would choose. Somehow my sister and I had this weird internal tracking device that would invariably pick out the most expensive pastry in the case, no matter how demure it appeared. And of course, my father being familiar with this type of aesthetic affliction would let us point out which delicacy we wanted without ever once saying no.

He was awesome that way. I suppose he was always trying to shelter us from reality, never once letting on to how much or how little cash he actually had in his wallet.

Our appreciation for quality began to sprout early in our lives under the capable tutelage of my father. As Nene and I got older, we were both able to zero in on the most outrageously expensive piece of anything we were looking at, whether it was shoes, jewelry, artwork, antiques, whatever. Our homing device would automatically target that one piece that would be in the hundreds or thousands, and we would crack up laughing and say, "Yep, Papi would definitely want us to buy that." On occasion this ability served us well and at other times made our lives a bit more complicated and challenging.

Once we had all our treasures packaged in the glossy white box with Vannie Tilden embossed lettering and tied securely with a fancy black-and-white checkered ribbon, we were good to go. We waved goodbye to the kind ladies at the counter and thanked them politely. As we quietly exited the bakery with our glossy white box in tow, there was a bit of reverence in our demeanor. I suppose we knew what a priceless gift our father had given us. He was teaching us life lessons in the most unusual ways.

To an average person, a trip to a pastry shop would have been no big deal, rather ho-hum in fact. But to us, knowing these types of gestures from our father did not come without a financial sacrifice, we realized reverence was the only appropriate reaction to have. With the grace of two gazelles, we entered the car and held our breath all the way home until we could deliver the tasty treasures to our family.

As we came into the kitchen with our package, everyone wanted to see what we'd picked out at the bakery. And all we did was look. We didn't eat our pastries until early afternoon when we had our *merienda*, better known as an afternoon snack. We began learning about delayed gratification at an early age. Finally the hour of la merienda would roll around, and my mom would bring out all the treats, serving my dad his pecan roll with black coffee and our treats with glasses of cold milk. We would quietly savor each and every bite, all the while taking in the aroma of the rich vanilla bean icing or the intensity of the dark and semi-sweet chocolate flavors.

As I said, a trip to Vannie Tilden might not sound like an extraordinary event or outing. But to me, my father's gesture opened our eyes to different possibilities. These simple experiences took us out of our everyday world, a world that didn't know what a cream puff was. It opened our lives to a different language, culture, and lifestyle. I'm not quite sure if this was his intention, but it was the end result.

None of us remained in South Texas. We all ventured far away from our childhood hometown. But we definitely took with us many happy memories and a strong sense of cultural identity and history. Somehow we were all destined to live in a bigger pond. We figured it was just one more thing our father would have wanted us to do, find the biggest pond we could and jump right in.

Las Cazuelas

IT WAS THE BEGINNING OF SUMMER. I had finished first grade and was as free as a bird. Just how I liked it.

That first night of my summer vacation was always the sweetest night of the summer for me. I went to bed with the biggest grin on my face, knowing I would be able to sleep late the next day and the next day and lots of days after that. I would take my time rolling out of bed in the morning and take even more time eating my breakfast before going outside to play all day with the other neighborhood kids. What a great carefree feeling. The only thing I was responsible for was to have all the fun I could cram into three months of summer vacation.

Because we'd all done so well on our report cards, my father wanted to reward us with a special night out on the town. He decided we would drive across the bridge from Brownsville into Matamoros, the small town on the Mexican side of the Rio Grande, and dine at Las Cazuelas, one of his favorite restaurants. That sounded so sophisticated to me. I was the youngest of five, and everything sounded sophisticated and grown-up.

We dressed nicely for dinner but kept it simple due to the intense summer heat. If you have ever been in Brownsville during the summer, you know how hot and humid it gets. You could rarely make it out of the shower and dry off without working up a sticky sweat all over again. So my sister and I wore simple cotton blouses that would breathe and shorts with a pair of Keds, while my older sisters and brother dressed more formally.

As usual, our parents wanted this to be a special treat, so our first stop was at the plaza, or town square. There was a similar layout in many Mexican towns and villages: lining the central plaza was at least one cathedral, a few smaller churches, shops, and restaurants. You always found a gazebo in the center where there would often be a band playing at night. It was the perfect place to take your family for an outing. The plaza had a park-like feeling with abundant shade trees, benches, and beautiful flowers. There were street vendors selling all kinds of wonderful food to eat, toys, trinkets, and souvenirs for the tourists.

We strolled around the perimeter of the plaza, talking about how well we had done in school and about all the things we wanted to do during the summer. Mostly we would play outdoors with all the neighborhood kids. Nothing elaborate, just have fun by exercising our imaginations. Papi told us that we would have our yearly visit to my grandmother's house in Nuevo Laredo sometime in early July. We would be able to stay for as long as my granny, Bueli, and aunt, Tía Lolis, could stand to have us around.

I sincerely looked forward to spending time with my granny and aunt. They always spoiled us and made sure we had fun. Tía Lolis had never been able to have children of her own, so we were the lucky recipients of her undivided and undiluted attentions. There wasn't anything Tía wouldn't do for us. How I loved that! Visiting in July also meant that I would have my birthday at Bueli's house, and you have no idea how special that would be unless you had been there to experience it firsthand.

After our family did several laps around the plaza, I suppose my parents felt we were exhausted enough to take us to the restaurant for the dining portion of our evening.

Las Cazuelas was a quaint restaurant tucked away on a side street in a tree-lined residential neighborhood. The only clue that this was a restaurant was the brightly hand-painted sign that hung above the front door. It simply read: *Las Cazuelas, Bienvenidos* (The Cooking Pots, Welcome). Cazuelas are glazed terra cotta pots used for cooking food. These types of pots are an essential element for the traditional Mexican kitchen. Cooking in cazuelas always gives the food a signature flavor.

At the entrance of the restaurant were rustic, wooden, double doors that looked antique. As my dad herded his brood to the entrance, he pushed the doors open, revealing a rectangular-shaped courtyard. High walls made of brick and concrete surrounded the courtyard that kept the street noise out while making it cool and private.

It was not at all what I was expecting.

The maître d' eagerly escorted us to a table large enough to seat our family of seven. The metal folding chairs had the Carta Blanca beer logo printed on the back. A crisply starched white tablecloth dressed the table, along with neatly pressed red linen dinner napkins, crystal water goblets, and more silverware than I knew what to do with.

Our waiter helped the ladies with their chairs and then began taking orders for drinks. We had worked up quite a thirst during our stroll around the plaza. I ordered my favorite *refresco, agua de tamarindo.* This was a refreshing drink made from tamarind, sugar, water, and ice. My sister sitting next to me ordered *agua de sandia*, which was a similar drink made with watermelon. Everyone else ordered *refrescos* made from either fresh pineapple or guava. My dad opted for a cold Carta Blanca beer. Then there was my oldest sister who probably thought she was too sophisticated to have a fruit drink so she ordered an ice-cold Coca-Cola.

By sundown, the evening air began to feel a bit chilly, making me wish I hadn't worn shorts. As the waiters quietly lit the outdoor torches, the light softened to an amber glow, and with the soothing sound of the trickling fountain in the courtyard, I began to nod off.

Suddenly, out of nowhere, a band of strolling mariachis appeared. They began going from table to table playing classic *charro* music. It was so festive and loud that I promptly got my second wind and was wide-awake. Papi had gone ahead and ordered an appetizer for all of us to share, a huge bowl of the most delicious guacamole I had ever tasted. It was spicy with finely chopped jalapeño chili peppers and a little tart from lime juice that had been drizzled on top. The bowl went around the table one time, which was enough guacamole to take the edge off our hunger.

The next course was individual cups of steaming *frijoles borrachos,* or drunken beans, so named because the beans are cooked with beer. The frijoles borrachos from Las Cazuelas still top my list of the best beans I've ever eaten. They used just the right amounts of onions, garlic, salt, fresh cilantro, tomatoes, and serrano peppers and added a chunk of ham. Then there was the beer, of course, that gave the beans their distinctive flavor and name. But I think part of the big secret to the unique taste had to be the cazuelas in which the beans were cooked. The drunken beans came with soft hand-pressed corn tortillas that had a subtle grilled flavor.

Great care and attention to detail were taken in the food preparation, and that was part of the charm of Las Cazuelas.

The time finally came for us to place our orders for the main course. You wouldn't think I'd still have room for more food, but I did.

Papi told us that we could order anything we wanted from the menu and to place our own orders with the waiter.

As far as I was concerned, that was the real reward for making good grades. I was going to be able to act like the older kids. For the first time ever, my mom didn't have to ask me what I wanted to order. Nope, I could tell the waiter myself. I was thrilled. It made me feel like I had gone up a notch in kid status, and I definitely felt proud. I loved how Papi made these small gestures that made me feel special.

The waiter arrived and began to take our dinner orders. He started on the opposite side of the table where my oldest sister sat and slowly made his way around to our side. It felt like it took hours for him to make it back to our end of the table. Being the youngest, I was the last person at the table to order. Just as my stomach let out a loud growl, the waiter swiveled around to face me.

"*¿Bueno, señorita, que quieres ordenar esta noche?*" he asked. (Well, miss, what do you wish to order tonight?)

I proudly held up my menu and said loudly and very clearly, "*Una orden de calambres, por favor.*" (I will have an order of *calambres* please.) I felt a sense of accomplishment with how well I had placed my order. And I had said it all in Spanish.

Well with that, all hell broke loose. Everyone at the table started to laugh so hard that some of them were in tears within seconds, including the waiter who was by this time holding onto his jiggling stomach. Even my traitor parents were laughing at me or at what I had said, or well, I wasn't quite sure what they were laughing at. I had no clue. I started to think maybe I had done something foolish or said something inappropriate and began to feel self-conscious. I felt stupid not knowing what had happened and why everyone was howling so loudly. My big brown eyes started to fill up with tears, and my lower lip slowly started to quiver.

My sister, Nene, yelled at my mom, "Come quick, Mami. Paty is going to cry."

With that SOS, my mom came running over to me, put her arms around me, and held me tight. The rescue hug automatically made me feel even more pathetic, and I started to sob.

My mom tried to explain why everyone was laughing so hard, in between trying to stifle her own giggles. She said no one was trying to be mean or hurt my feelings. That was the one thing she wanted me to understand. What I had said was so hilarious they couldn't help laughing.

Apparently when the waiter asked for my order, I politely and in a very mature voice had ordered *calambres*, which are actually leg-cramps. You know the ones I'm talking about, a charley horse. What I had wanted to order was *alambres*. That means shish kebab. Oops. I guess that was pretty funny.

Can you imagine how the poor waiter must have felt having this cute little girl chime in that she would like an order of leg cramps? What else could you do but laugh hysterically?

Was that experience humbling? You bet. Was it the end of the world? Nope. Did it help me see how important it was to be able to laugh at myself and not take things so personally? Yes, it did.

Dinner that evening at Las Cazuelas was very memorable for me. My dad took us to celebrate something special, and we did. We celebrated my first experience of being the butt of a joke, of sorts. That might have been the first time, but it certainly would not be the last.

Armadillo World Headquarters

How does the saying go? If you can remember the sixties, then you probably weren't there.

Yet, if you'd experienced the scene at a beer garden called Armadillo World Headquarters in Austin, Texas, in the early seventies, you'd probably be saying, "Wasn't that far-out—the Armadillo, the music, the food, the beer, all the cool people, so perfect?" Had you been there, sitting in the beer garden, enjoying your cold Lone Star beer with an order of nachos, listening to the latest local band, looking up at the peachy-golden sunset sky, and feeling the gentle breeze blowing through the garden, you would remember it. Trust me.

For me it was all about being young, beautiful, and free spirited. Though I was intent on learning all I could from my university classes, I was hoping to fill in some of the blank spaces in my education with full-throttle life experiences . . . such as listening to some of the best progressive Austin bands around. The sound, in later years, became as iconic to the Armadillo as it is now to the Austin music scene and Austin City Limits on the Public Broadcasting

Station. It was a moment in time when being a hippie in Austin was a really cool thing.

I was a voracious reader back then and still am. There wasn't a philosophy book, novel, or nonfiction book I didn't pick up and read. Wanting to get out of my head a bit and have a mind-altering experience firsthand, I decided that a visit to the Armadillo would be perfect.

Sitting in the beer garden for the very first time with my friend Benjamin was memorable. I can still remember what I wore, how magnetic I felt, and what we talked about as we ordered our pitcher of beer and nachos.

The admission price for an actual concert at the Armadillo was affordable to most people. But to a starving college student, the only affordable thing was sitting outside the concert hall in the beer garden. I was content with my surroundings, happy to feel the night breezes against my taut tanned skin, drink my beer, eat my nachos, and listen to the music as it pulsated through the walls.

The beer was served in huge, chilled glass pitchers and was relatively cheap. That was good because I was drinking much faster than my date. The cold beer seemed to keep my cheeks from blushing. I could feel my body temperature rise as my friend would lean over and brush away, ever so gently, a stubborn strand of my hair that would fall in front of my face. He was so good-looking—the kind of good-looking that made a shy girl like me blush every time he said my name.

His eyes were the color of an Austin summer sky, a pale cerulean blue. His hair was light brown with red and blond sun-kissed highlights. Tall and lean, he wore the tightest Levi's I had ever seen on a guy. Those jeans were tight in all the right places. He was wearing weathered black-and-tan cowboy boots and a well-worn cowboy hat that made him way too appealing. His thick beard accented the long, straight hair that hung halfway down his back. He was almost too pretty to look at . . . almost.

Whenever I became uncomfortable gazing into his chiseled face, I would pick up my mug of beer, take a swig, and eat more nachos. Then he would start talking philosophy, which he knew excited me. With the philosophizing swirling around me like a dizzying wind, I began to blush again, so I took another swig of beer and ate more nachos. The more nachos I ate, the more I started to think about how great the nachos looked. They were perfect, on that perfect night, in that perfect setting, with that perfect guy.

What was it about the nachos anyway? (What was it about the guy?) I started to think about it, and taking a good look at the nachos, I thought they seemed simple enough. Why their strong appeal? What was the attraction? Was it the homemade corn tortilla chips that had been fried at just the right temperature to make them light and crispy, not oily and heavy like most of the chips you get at faux Mexican restaurants? These were what tortilla chips should be like all over the world, I mused. The cook might have dusted them lightly with a little kosher salt, but that was it. Then there was the smallest piece of sharp cheddar cheese melted to the bubbling point on every chip, and each nacho was individually topped with a slice of jalapeño. How did they do that? Wouldn't it be too time-consuming, placing one slice at a time on each chip, I pondered.

Just then, as I was getting lost in my nacho thoughts, Benjamin grabbed my hand playfully and asked me to please dance with him on the side of the stage where some of the lesser-known bands would play. Electricity shot right through my hand, coursed through the length of my arm, and went straight to my heart . . . and then I gulped. "Well, maybe in a few minutes, after I chill out a little more with another . . . glass of beer." I quickly pulled my hand out of his grip, got a passing waiter to stop, and told him, "Hey, could you send another round to our table? And maybe another order of nachos too?"

The cute waiter chuckled, glanced at my flushed cheeks, and said, "Sure, man, whatever you want."

"Cool," I mumbled to the waiter. I had gotten myself out of that awkward moment without a hitch.

Then Benjamin whispered in my ear, "Hey, we can eat, LATER. Let's just get up and feel the music coursing through our bodies, babe."

I really didn't like the way he melodiously whispered, "Feel the music coursing through our bodies." I felt that hot flashing kind of thing going on with my cheeks again as he looked directly into my eyes, causing my blushing to go from warm pink to hot pink to bright fuchsia.

What was I going to do now? The most beautiful man I had ever been on a date with was hitting on me. And why shouldn't he be, my ego responded. I was an irresistible twenty-one-year-old girl in snug hip-hugger bell-bottom jeans with a form-fitting, red cowgirl shirt that had mother-of-pearl snap buttons down the front.

As if on cue, our second pitcher of beer arrived at the table, along with our second order of bubbling-hot cheesy nachos.

As the music seemed to get louder and louder and other couples jumped up to "feel the music course through their bodies," I began to wonder what was more fascinating, the beer, the nachos, or Benjamin. Well, that thought seemed to flash by as soon as it had entered my mind. I took another swig of beer and bite of nachos. Oh yeah, did I mention that the nachos had just the right amount of cheese and jalapeños to match every swig of beer I took?

I liked the way the vibrations of the bass guitar and drums made my body feel alive. The sounds vibrated through my ears. They also entered through my feet that were touching the ground and through the pores on my body and through my eyes when I noticed how Benjamin was swaying to the music and through all the smoke that was circling around us. All the smoke . . . smoke? Where was all the smoke coming from? Oh, is that a super-sized nacho with a monster slab of cheese and mutant jalapeño slice on the edge of the platter? Boy, I'd better grab that one before Benjamin does. Ah, that was so tasty.

I couldn't remember when I'd had such a nice time at an outdoor garden restaurant. Well, except for the time my folks took us to dine at Las Cazuelas when I was a little kid. I took another swig of beer and ate a few more nachos. Suddenly I became aware that I was the only one eating nachos and drinking beer. Benjamin was just sitting there, staring into space, shaking his head, and letting a few muted chuckles escape from his full lips.

I remember thinking that he was acting weird, and I was starting to feel uncomfortable and embarrassed.

Suddenly he said, "Hey, beautiful, come on and dance with me. The night is perfect, and you look perfect, and I want us to remember this as our perfect first date. What do you say?"

Trying to shake the cobwebs out of my head, I said, "Huh? The music is too loud. I can't hear you." Then I saw the same cute waiter go by.

Moments later he came up to our table and said, "Can I get you two another pitcher, more nachos? Or anything else? Anything?"

And I said, "Huh? Where's all the smoke coming from?"

The waiter didn't respond.

"Benjamin," I yelled through the music, "are you having a good time?" Don't ask me why I said that, but I did. That was an inane thing to say. Without giving him a chance to answer, I bellowed, "I sure am! I love the beer, and these nachos are the best in the world; I'm sure of it. I'll never forget how good these nachos taste. Never." I felt so peaceful after blurting my declaration of love for the nachos that I let out a deep and profound sigh. I could've sworn I saw Benjamin rolling his eyes after I sighed.

After a few awkward moments, Benjamin finally spoke. "You know what, babe? I think I'm going to call it a night. You seem to be having a great time. Stay. I'll see you in class next week. Save me a seat. Here's some money for you to take a cab home, okay? And . . . you're beautiful. You know that, don't you, babe?" Then he held my face in his big soft hands and planted a sweet and gentle kiss on my lips.

Next thing I knew, Benjamin was paying the tab and heading towards the door, and I mumbled to myself, "What was that all about? What just happened?"

I felt bad for Benjamin because the music just kept getting better and so did all the smoke around us. Stopping with the beer and nachos, I just sat there taking it all in, wondering if this evening qualified as a full-throttle life experience.

As my gorgeous date walked out the exit, shaking his head, our cute waiter walked up to my table. He leaned in and said that he'd just gotten off his shift and wondered if I'd like to go in to hear the band play and maybe smoke a joint with him.

Smiling back at him, I said, "Well, maybe in a few minutes after I chill out a little more."

I was left wondering if the pot smoke had anything to do with how good the food tasted. But it really didn't matter. What I'd decided right then and there was that you can always hook up with a perfect date but you can't always hook up with a perfect nacho.

La Fiesta

IT WAS THE MONTH OF JULY, and I was eight years old. My sister Nene and I were staying with my grandmother, Bueli, and my aunt for part of our summer vacation. They lived in a very humble neighborhood in Nuevo Laredo, which is across the border from Laredo, Texas.

Although my granny and my aunt didn't have much money and lived in a modest house, I never thought of them as being poor. Their lives always seemed full and happy. I felt sure they were actually very rich, and in many ways they were.

A white picket fence lined the front of their tidy yard. Bueli displayed her prized rose bushes and brilliant red poinsettias in the front yard not only for her own enjoyment but also for her neighbors. Suspended from the eaves of the front porch were several baskets of donkey's tail, a succulent plant with petals the color of green grapes that hang down in clusters. On the north side of the house going towards her backyard was a narrow brick patio the length of the house. Nailed to the concrete wall on the right were a dozen or so Christmas cactus plants in colorful hand-painted wall pockets. By Thanksgiving that wall would be a riot of colors that would last past Christmas and into the New Year.

BUELI IN THE FRONT YARD, SO PROUD OF HER
RED POINSETTIA PLANTS IN WINTER'S FULL BLOOM.

The backyard was much larger than the front yard. There were lots of fruit trees including citrus, peach, and three types of figs. In the middle of the yard was a huge concrete slab, or so it seemed to me when I was young.

This was the area where my aunt, Tía Lolis, would stage her incredible summertime parties. She would string up colorful lights, bring her record player from the house out to the patio, and place metal folding chairs all around the dance floor. She would cook several of her signature dishes and invite her co-workers from the bank, and they would in turn bring along their boyfriends, cousins, brothers, or sisters. Each group came carrying several platters of food. By the time all the guests had arrived, the table by the bar area was filled end to end with exotic culinary masterpieces, some of which I had never tasted.

The gathering of friends and family expanded as the evening wore on. It was really fun watching so many people mingle, tell silly jokes, and dance. Eventually the eating would begin in earnest, only to be followed by the drinking of rum and Coke, then dancing a few *cumbias*, starting up a conga line, and definitely lots of laughing. It felt as though I had stumbled onto the set of a classic Hollywood movie starring Katherine Hepburn and Cary Grant.

My eyes felt like they were twinkling, reflecting the beacon of light that surrounded my aunt. She was always happy, and her huge smile and great disposition drew people to her.

On the night of this fiesta, my aunt took Nene and me aside and said she was going to trust us to be on our very best behavior with all her guests. We could eat whatever we wanted, drink however many sodas we wanted, and stay up as late as we wanted as long as we did one thing for her—make sure any hats, wraps, jackets, and purses her guests brought were laid neatly on the bed in her bedroom. Nothing was to get crinkled or wrinkled or tangled. "Understand?" she cooed.

"Yup, we heard you loud and clear, Tía. You can trust us," we both chimed. That was it. That was our only job assignment. Simple.

Our fun really began as we started to sample the food. We ate until we thought we might get sick. We took a break from our grazing and rested, watching the couples dance for a while. Eventually we stood up for round two of our gluttony.

I was most fond of my aunt's *gorditas*. They are similar to a corn tortilla but much thicker and smaller in size. She would pinch the edges, making a lip about a quarter inch high and then spread them with hot green salsa or refried black beans with crumbled *queso fresco*. They were topped with thinly sliced lettuce drizzled with fresh Mexican cream. My sister always went for the grilled corn on the cob that is slathered in butter and then sprinkled with hot chili powder and a squeeze of lemon juice. This type of food experience is something you never forget.

The party progressed with great gusto. And we continued to savor all the food with gusto too, until my sister and I did a naughty thing. When no one was looking, we began helping ourselves to the punch that was apparently spiked with rum. Neither one of us could remember if Tía had told us the punch was off limits. I thought she had, but we convinced ourselves that she probably wouldn't mind because it was just punch, right? The problem wasn't that we had indulged in one cup of punch. No . . . the problem was that we lost track of how many cups of punch we had. We brazenly plowed through countless cups. Pretty soon Nene looked at me and started laughing and pointing at me and said, "You have two heads. No, wait. You have three heads."

I instantly starting laughing right back at her and said, "No, you have two heads. No, wait. You have three heads and four arms."

Laughing harder than either of us had ever laughed, we began to stumble in the direction of the kitchen door. It was totally dark outside with only a hint of light radiating from the festive and colorful lights that hung above the dance floor. Nene walked through the kitchen door into the house, with me on her coattails, zigzagging all over the place. She extended her arms out in front of her for balance and promptly knocked over an empty water jug. There were several close calls after that. She came within inches of knocking over Bueli's glass figurines, Tía's perfume bottles, and the little wire birdcage that housed one of Bueli's canaries. I was so scared that we were going to get caught and punished that I started to sweat like a little piglet. Stumbling through my granny's house in the dark felt as dangerous as walking through a minefield. The only thing that kept me from causing a disaster was the ribbon on the back of my sister's dress that I was clinging to for dear life. "Watch out, Nene. We're going to blow up!"

She let out a shriek, "Blow up? No, I don't want to blow up." Then she started to cry.

The last thing I remember after Nene started to cry was that we both landed with a huge thud on top of my aunt's bed. On top of all those nice hats, jackets, wraps, and purses that my aunt had strictly told us not to crinkle, wrinkle, or tangle. Oh well, we were hopelessly glued to her bed. Neither one of us could move a muscle. And then everything went blank as we both passed out.

The next morning came way too soon. Bueli began stomping around the living room where we were sleeping. Then I heard her banging around in the kitchen. Then banging around in the dining room, then banging around again in the kitchen. Dear Lord, make her stop, I silently prayed. Next, Bueli came barreling through the living room again like a freight train and yelled out to my aunt who was only two inches away from her, "¿Gustas café?" Why was she yelling at my aunt about drinking coffee right now? It didn't even look like the sun had come up yet. I had forgotten what early risers they were, usually in bed by 8 p.m. and up by 5 a.m. Ugh. I just wanted to keep the covers over my head. Of course, my sister, who could sleep through a hurricane, was sound asleep and letting out a delicate snore every so often.

That's the moment when Bueli exacted the punishment for last night's bad behavior. "*Niñas, levántense. Tiempo para el desayuno.*" (Girls, get up. It's time for breakfast.)

She dragged us out of bed right there on the spot. My sister started to cry and said she felt sick and wanted to stay in bed. Well, that wasn't going to happen. Bueli made us both get up and go sit at the breakfast table and then brought us a tall glass of warm milk, tortillas with scrambled eggs, and refried beans. My aunt and granny joined us at the table. They both proceeded to eat their breakfast as we stared at them in horror. Neither one of them ever said a word to us about the night before. They really didn't have to. We knew we had done wrong. I'm sure they must have been disappointed with our behavior at the party, but I'm also pretty certain they'd seen way worse from our older siblings. At least that's what I kept telling myself all throughout breakfast. Girls will be girls, right?

We moved the food around our plates and kept cutting the pieces of egg into tiny ones to make it look like we had eaten some. Finally, Bueli told us to get dressed because it was Sunday and she thought it would be nice if we all went to early mass. "Dear Lord," I thought, "make her stop."

Off we went to the bathroom to bathe and get dressed. By six thirty, we were heading out the door. Nene and I were trailing a few feet behind them. Every couple of minutes, Bueli would look over her shoulder to check on us and then wave at us to speed it up and not lag behind.

We made it to the bus stop a few blocks from their house and waited for the bus going to town. After a ten-minute wait, it finally appeared, and we hopped on the crowded bus and rode for twenty minutes on a very bumpy road filled with potholes. Every time the bus hit a pothole, it shook violently because it most likely didn't have any shock absorbers. All four tires were probably bald, too.

LOOKING ANGELIC AND ABSOLVED.

I was sweating all over the place. I'm sure I looked horrible. As I glanced out the window, I caught my reflection in the window, and it looked exactly like a zombie with a hangover. My bangs were stuck to my forehead, and my braids were stuck to my neck. The biggest problem was that I had always been prone to motion sickness. In fact, I still am. I'm always the first person to get carsick and will often have to hurl one mile into a road trip. Well I was pretty certain that at any second, all those wonderful dishes we had savored the night before and all that tasty punch we had inhaled were going to make a command performance right on my granny's lap. Bueli saw that I was all slumped over, and she told me to sit up straight and to quit slouching. At the risk of sounding redundant, I repeated what had now become my mantra, "Dear Lord, make her stop."

And just as soon as I had voiced my silent prayer, we arrived at our destination, and we were herded off the bus. I thought I looked bad with a pale face and dark circles under my eyes until I caught sight of my sister. Her face was every shade of green you can think of and some you never could have imagined. Once we caught sight of each other and how bad we looked, we both started to laugh in spite of ourselves. Our heads hurt every time we laughed, but we couldn't help it.

We filed into the big cathedral behind Bueli and Tía. Nene and I scooped up some holy water and splashed it all over our faces, necks, and arms. It was a cooling tonic on our bodies, helping the nausea recede. Tía raised an eyebrow and gasped when she saw us do this and told us we weren't birds and that wasn't water in a birdbath. Oops.

The next thing that happened was a real miracle. My aunt had me sit next to her, and my sister sat next to my granny. They told us both to lie down on the pew and go to sleep, that God would understand. They took off the light shawls they were wearing and covered us up. After they did that, they both winked at us and chuckled. We both fell asleep and did not wake up until mass was over and the whole congregation had left the church. They gave us each a gentle nudge, and we woke up feeling so much better, as if all our transgressions from the night before had been miraculously erased.

As I walked out of the church, I felt like a different person. I wasn't feeling the least bit sick; in fact, I felt great. So did my sister. We walked from the church to the plaza in the center of town and strolled along at a leisurely pace. The plaza was already filled with lots of families with children playing everywhere and dozens of street vendors selling all kinds of local dishes, balloons, gardenia corsages for the ladies, cut flowers, musical instruments, wooden puppets, stuffed toys, and more. As we came up to each vendor, we would check out what he was selling and ask what the prices were; then we'd walk to the next vendor and do the same thing over again. It was fun looking at all the colorful carts and the unique items they sold. And the food carts were my favorite; the food was similar to Bueli's home cooking. The longer we strolled, the stronger the aromas became, and within the hour we were all starving.

We came to a vendor that was selling hot tamales, gorditas, and roasted corn on the cob. Bueli asked if we were ready for some lunch. We both nodded our heads yes. She was glad to see that we'd gotten our appetites back, winked, and tugged on one of my braids, and my aunt tussled my sister's bangs.

I ordered the gorditas, hoping they would taste as good as the ones my aunt had made, and my sister grabbed an ear of corn. Tía and Bueli bought a dozen tamales, some with beans, some with pork, and some sweet ones with raisins.

They figured we had miraculously found our appetites.

First Street Bakery

"*VÁMONOS, MUCHACHITAS*," I HEARD ECHO THROUGH my foggy dream state. "*Vámonos, se nos va hacer tarde.*"

I struggled to pull myself out of a beautiful dream I was having. In the dream I could see myself standing at the edge of a jetty with my toes hanging over, getting splashed by the ocean spray. There was a cool misty breeze blowing with waves crashing below and seagulls circling above me in the sky. Towards the horizon, shrimp boats were heading further out to sea. I could even hear the bell ringing from a buoy, bobbing around in the waves off in the distance. It felt so peaceful, so soothing. Then something began jolting me out of this reverie. I heard repeated calls from what sounded like a drill sergeant say, "Come on, little girls. . . . Come on, we're going to be late." What little girls? And late for what?

No sooner did I have that thought than I felt someone trying to tickle me awake. "Stop it," I whined. My sister had accomplished her mission to wake me up when the yelling from my dad had failed.

It was Sunday morning, early Sunday morning, around

six o'clock. Who on earth would want to wake up their kids at that inhumane hour? My dad would, that's who. He did it for our continued education in the appreciation of the finer things in life, like being the first person in line at the most well-known local Mexican bakery in town.

Papi was dressed and ready to head out the door and reminded us that time was of the essence. Getting up early to go to the bakery had lost its appeal for our older siblings a few years earlier. That meant Nene and I, being the youngest in the family, would carry the torch of tradition with our dad.

We headed into town, across the railroad tracks to the First Street Bakery. Anyone who was serious about *pan dulce* would get to the bakery early because the best pastry would sell out right away. I suspected there was another reason that my dad liked to be there early. His ulterior motives may have been the real reason he'd hit the road by six thirty in the morning.

Mexican pastry is called *pan dulce* (sweet bread). The irony of it is that most of the Mexican style pastry is hardly sweet at all and definitely not overly rich. Each type of sweet bread has its own name like *conchas* (shells), *marranitos* (little pigs), *empanadas* (turnovers filled with pumpkin, coconut, or pineapple), *polvorones* (crumbling cookies), *cuernos* (horns), *campechanas* (puff pastries), some glazed pastry that looked like angel wings, and many more.

Mexican sweet bread is simple, plain, and very tasty. The fact that it isn't overly sweet means it is versatile. You can have it with a cup of coffee in the morning or have it for breakfast with some refried beans smeared on top, which is just how I liked it. Of course, I loved refried beans on almost anything; I couldn't help myself.

Conchas are round, lightly raised breads with a top that looks similar to a shell. They came with a creamy white, yellow, pink, or chocolate topping. I used to love having a concha after school for a snack with refried beans. Sounds weird I'm sure, but it had that whole sweet and savory thing going on.

First Street Bakery was the most quaint, quirky, and rundown little old building you'd ever seen. It looked like it had originally been a regular house that was later converted into a bakery. The building was painted white, or at least the paint that hadn't peeled off was white. There were two rickety wooden steps in front of the double doors. Upon entering, you were greeted by the noisy screen doors that opened into the bakery.

I remember thinking the double doors were great because the back door at our house, which opened out to the carport and was used more often than the front door, was a single screen door. There would be a huge bottleneck of kids getting arms and legs in a tangle trying to be the first one out the door just to get dibs on a window seat in my dad's car. I thought that a double door like the one at the First Street Bakery would have been a handy renovation for that kitchen door. It's a pity I was so young with such great architectural vision and no carpentry skills.

At the bakery, both screen doors would open and close with each customer's arrival and departure, creating a horrendously squeaky bang that reverberated in the air for a long time. It was a distinctive sound . . . one that was authentically rustic, down home, and a little annoying. I suppose the owners never considered oiling the hinges.

Upon entering, you'd see a single pastry case that spanned the width of the entire room. On the wall to the right of the pastry case was a chalkboard listing each item with its corresponding price: different types of pan dulce, tortillas either corn or white flour, pan *blanco* (similar to a crusty baguette), pan *francés* (French bread). Then there was the current day's price for my dad's "ulterior motive" on the board, written in huge hot-pink letters: *Barbacoa, 59¢/la libra* (Mexican barbecue, 59¢ per pound).

My poor dad was always trying to expose us to unique cultural experiences such as barbacoa. He loved his barbacoa so much that getting up early in the morning and hauling us down there with him was something he genuinely enjoyed. That was his Sunday treat, his only Sunday treat, and barbacoa was something I dreaded.

Do you even know what goes into Mexican barbecue? Well, I'll tell you and I won't mince words. It's everything that comes from a cow's head and then is slow-cooked in an outdoor pit. It's plain too, not at all like American style barbecue with a sweet-'n'-spicy sauce. No sauce to disguise the taste . . . just the contents of a cow's head. I mean the brains, the eyeballs, the cheeks, and the tongue. Sound tasty? Maybe if you had a mature palette and liked exotic cultural foods from around the world, you might've thought this would be something to sample, wrapped up in a warm homemade corn tortilla.

Normally my dad would get an order of tongue and cheek, but I suspect on occasion, he'd get some of the more graphic parts. No matter how many times I tried to eat some of the tongue, I couldn't keep it down. I would heap tons of salt on it in a feeble attempt to disguise the flavor and then wrap it up in a corn tortilla. I never failed to gag and come close to throwing up. On occasion I would try the cheek too because that was the closest thing to my mom's roast beef. But I always got the same gag reflex. The aroma of rancid grease filled my nostrils. It was a funky smell. I ended up becoming vegetarian at age twenty-four and I still am to this day. Not sure if that barbacoa exposure had anything to do with it, but there you have it.

To please my dad after he'd gone to all the trouble of taking us with him to the bakery and letting us pick out all our favorite pan dulce, it seemed only fair to try some of his type of comfort food. I'm not sure if all kids have trouble at the beginning with barbacoa, but my sister and I sure did. The older kids were able to eat it, but I don't think they had the same gusto as my dad. I can't remember ever seeing my mom eat any, but maybe she did.

As I said earlier, First Street Bakery was not at all like the other well-known bakery in town, Vannie Tilden, which specialized in elaborate wedding cakes and fancy pastries filled with creams, custards, and chocolate. When we went to VT, no one ever asked us if we wanted cow tongue or cow brains or corn tortillas. But at First Street Bakery, they did. And that is exactly what made it unique and authentic.

It was my dad's ability to go between worlds and enjoy each one for the best it had to offer that helped make me who I am today. I'm sure he would never have taken the credit for it.

He never cared if we didn't eat the barbacoa or the *menudo* or the duck or the oysters or the *cabrito en sangre* (baby goat in blood) . . . or even the disgusting creation he made me try at a five-star restaurant in Mexico City. It had a cylindrical shape and was wrapped in what looked like vermicelli. To my gastronomical horror, the dish was chopped-up tripe wrapped in thin strips of tripe, all pan seared until crispy golden.

It was being open to try new things that mattered to him. Getting us out of our comfort zone in order to help us expand our horizons was his mission and ultimately his one and only ulterior motive.

I figured as long as we learned to keep those double screen doors of our minds wide open, we'd do just fine.

House of Tiles, Mexico City
Casa de los Azulejos

During the summer of my sixteenth year and my sister's nineteenth, my mother, sister, and I spent our vacation visiting our father who was working in Mexico City at the time. He had rented a three-bedroom apartment in a ritzy building with a doorman, elevator, and million-dollar view.

The first sound we heard every morning from our sixth-floor apartment on Insurgentes Norte was traffic. It lulled you to sleep at night and would abruptly wake you in the morning with perhaps a speeding ambulance or a police siren. It was a sound you always heard. Honking horns, speeding cars, trucks, buses, taxis . . . a constant flow of traffic . . . a city teeming with life and activity. The traffic noise lightened up a bit in the wee hours of the morning but was always there in the background and would pick up in volume by mid-morning and reach a full crescendo by afternoon rush hour. After a couple of weeks of listening to the traffic, it became white noise, and I never had trouble sleeping. However, on my return home after summer vacation, it was the quiet that kept me up at night. It would take me a few weeks to readjust to the absence of the city traffic noise and embrace the soothing hum of an air-conditioner.

My morning routine in Mexico City was pretty much the same. I'd wake up, splash some cold water on my face, shuffle into our dining room, and look out the huge picture window. Looking across Insurgentes Norte toward downtown, I would begin to think about my day. If the sky was clear, I could see Popocatépetl, from our window. It was an active volcano that appeared far off in the distance but was only a few miles away. Also visible, standing tall and proud, was a skyscraper erected in the 1950s called La Torre Latino-Americana, the Latin-American Tower. Directly across the street from our apartment building was Ciudad Tlatelolco, Plaza de las Tres Culturas, a neighborhood that had been built around three different cultures—existing Aztec ruins including remains of a pyramid, an old church built by the Spanish invaders, and modern buildings built to encompass the other two. Pretty wild, huh?

As I stood there, glued to the window, taking it all in, Mami and my sister walked in from the kitchen. Nene spoke and yanked me out of my thoughts, "Hey, girlie-girl, we have a date to meet Carolina and her brother in the park later this morning. Did you forget, or do you need your *cafecito y pan dulce* to jolt your memory?"

"Yeah, I definitely need my coffee and sweet bread. You didn't eat all the *marranitos*, did you? I know how you are with those little marranitos. You just can't resist biting off their heads and feet," I responded, a bit annoyed. I had never been a chirpy morning-type person.

"If you'd just gotten up earlier, we wouldn't be having this conversation, would we?" she shot back.

Point taken.

I ventured into the kitchen and made myself a huge cup of *café Americano* with sweetened condensed milk to kickstart my morning. What to eat? I grabbed the last marranito and had to content myself with a pumpkin empanada as all the pineapple and coconut empanadas had vanished. My sister was right. Had I not still been lost in my thoughts, the choices would have been better.

I took my sweet bread back to the dining room table and proceeded to eat my breakfast. As I sat there savoring my pastry and looking out our picture window, which, by the way, took up the entire top half of the wall, I couldn't help but think about the past.

Ciudad Tlatelolco was the spot where there had recently been a student uprising in October of 1968, and many people, mostly college students, were gunned down by the military. The government and the military didn't want any protests. So they stopped it right away with a massacre. You could walk around the buildings and still see the bullet holes in the concrete buildings. Sad and very disturbing.

On more than one occasion, when we were returning to our apartment from the Súper-Mercado Aurrera, which was an enormous grocery store where we did most of our grocery shopping, some of the taxi drivers would refuse to drive through Ciudad Tlatelolco. What were they afraid of? The horrific events of the past? I didn't know.

So my mom, sister, and I would get out of the taxi and walk all the way back to our apartment, and I'm talking several very large city blocks, lugging all the bags of groceries. I didn't mind, though. I was a teenager living in one of the biggest cities in the world, and I loved everything about Mexico City. In spite of obvious signs that troubling changes were stirring in the wind, the city as a whole, at least for now, was still fairly innocent and relatively safe.

My sister snapped me out of my thoughts just then and said, "You'd better bite the head off your little pig pretty soon. If we don't leave the apartment within the next hour, we'll be late. We don't want to keep those guys waiting; that would be bad manners. We know better than to make people wait, don't we?"

"I know . . . enough already. I'm almost done with breakfast anyway, so don't worry. I'll be ready." Then I mumbled to myself, "Geeze," I was beginning to feel nagged.

We had made plans with Carolina, our local Mexican girlfriend, and her older brother, Ruben, the night before when they had called us from a party. They were sorry we'd missed it because there were so many handsome guys wanting to meet some *gringuitas*. You might note that, even though our parents were Mexican, making us 100 percent Mexican, the fact that we were born in Texas still made us *gringas* in their eyes and mysteriously more attractive. But, hey, every bit of leverage helped as far as I was concerned.

It was settled; we would meet in the historic and centrally located park called La Alameda and from there take a leisurely stroll to our favorite gathering place, Casa de los Azulejos (House of Tiles), to cook up more summer vacation plans with our friends.

I decided to wear the new dress my mom had made just before we left home. It was a pink-flowered, cotton pique, sleeveless dress, hemmed two inches above my knees. The design scooped in a bit at the shoulders, and the shorter length gave it a mod look; it made me feel trendy. I finished by running a brush through my hair and putting a lime-green headband on to keep the bangs off my face. This made my big brown eyes seem even larger. I grabbed my hot-pink, wooden-beaded shoulder bag and was ready to go.

My sister was waiting by the door, talking with my mom. We told her where we were headed and what time we'd be back. It was a simpler time when teenage girls traveling alone in the city were quite safe. We never gave it a second thought. Neither did our parents. Now I think to myself, that was just plain nuts! We still tease my ninety-year-old mom about it. She'd give us the one hundred pesos my dad had left for spending money, which was before the peso devaluations and a lot of money.

Eating out was relatively inexpensive, so we always felt rich. We'd walk from the apartment building one block to the street corner and start hailing cabs. There we were, a couple of teenage girls, flagging a cab in a city that was one of the largest in the world, and at present has more than twenty million inhabitants. Whatever we had to do to reach our final destination was worth it. I'd do it all over again in a heartbeat, just to sit one more time at the Casa de los Azulejos, sip my café Americano slowly, and absorb all the history and grandeur of the architecture and its untold stories.

The rendezvous point with our friends was always the same corner at La Alameda. As we walked through La Alameda, holding hands as they do in Mexico (not a custom we ever imitated in the United States), we marveled at all the fountains, statues, and monuments along the way. Mexico City was cosmopolitan in many ways. There were beautiful fountains all over the city. Traffic roundabouts on major streets such as Paseo de la Reforma would have a statue in the middle or a fountain or a fountain with a statue. Wherever you looked, there were cobblestone streets, gothic gargoyles perching from the top of buildings, classical statues, fountains, and monuments large and small, all incorporated into the landscape in a most natural way. Combined with its European influence were the ever-present remnants of the Aztec Empire.

The park itself was a patch of nature amid a massive metropolis. La Alameda is to Mexico City what Central Park is to New York City. Exactly. Benches are plentiful, as are people of all nationalities, children playing, vendors selling goods, tourists, the wealthy and the poorest of the poor.

That was another thing that was unique to my experience in Mexico City. The beggars were unfamiliar to my sanitized life back in Texas. What also surprised me were all the beautiful indigenous Indian women that were either trying to sell handmade crafts or were begging with their hands held out for any spare change you could give them. The ones with angelic babies swaddled in their *rebozos* (shawls) were the ones that always made me feel like crying and at the same time feel angry that this was our world . . . that a mother with a baby would be reduced to begging. I hated that. So I always carried lots of change around to give to those women. I'd also buy beaded work from them. Why give my money to a museum gift shop when I could pay the Indian artist directly? I was sheltered most of my youth, so this type of poverty was a bitter dose of reality.

It was early afternoon when we finally reached Casa de los Azulejos, which houses the famous Sanborns Café. It was perfect timing—the lunch crowd had come and gone, so the atmosphere was more relaxed. There were several Sanborns throughout Mexico, but the one inside Casa de los Azulejos was most famous. The whole dining experience was wonderful. Not just the food but also the mesmerizing tile work throughout the building and the impressive Baroque features of the architecture.

My tastes gravitated to traditional Mexican cuisine. And since I was too hungry to order from the pastry menu, I chose the lunch menu instead. I ordered *chilaquiles verdes* (a dish made with corn tortillas, lightly fried in fresh green chili and tomatillo sauce) that came with refried black beans topped with *queso ranchero* and a pineapple soda. That was perfection in my eyes.

Our orders were quite varied. Carolina preferred the *hamburguesa estilo Americano con papas fritas* (hamburger and French fries), Ruben generally had black coffee and a toasted *bolillo* (crusty French bread) with butter, and my sister had a piece of *pastel de tres leches* and *batido de nieve de vainilla* (three milks cake—a super-rich cake made with sweetened condensed milk, evaporated milk, and heavy cream—and a vanilla milkshake). I was always torn between the chilaquiles, the mole enchiladas, and their incredible milkshakes. But believe me, we came here often enough with my mom that I got to try out all my favorite dishes. In fact, any time we were in town running errands or sightseeing, we would use that as a legitimate excuse to eat at Sanborns Café in the House of Tiles. It became our favorite place to spend time with my mom, just us girls.

For some reason, meeting our metropolitan friends at the historic café made me feel sophisticated. The food I ordered was something an adult might order, not a teenager. We sat there for three hours, maybe more, eating and talking with hardly a break between sentences. Carolina caught us up on all the local news. She told us in animated detail about the party we'd missed the night before and gave us an outline of all the fiestas coming up in the next month. They had it all written down, times, places and who was giving the party. In turn, this information was passed on to our parents to see which parties we'd be allowed to attend. The entire list was rarely approved. I think forbidding some made my parents feel more engaged in our teenage life and maybe a bit more in control . . . you know, keeping the upper hand and keeping us guessing.

There we were, enjoying our afternoon at one of the best places on earth as far as I was concerned. Yes, Sanborns was a great café, but there were cafés everywhere. Part of the magic and the attraction was the greatness of the building itself. It had heart and soul. Do you know what I mean? There were glass doors throughout the three floors that looked out onto the street below, and the windows, doors, and balconies were all framed in carved stone. Inside, a courtyard with a fountain was surrounded by ornate stone columns, and a stone arch curved over the fountain. This was the seating area for the Sanborns Café. You could sit at either a table or a booth. The roof had stained glass over the courtyard area. All around were columns supporting the upper floors and an immense winding staircase. As I recall, we used to go up a dramatic staircase to use the ladies room on the second floor and check out the decorative and elaborate tile work that surrounded everything.

In case that was not enough to send us into sensory overload, there were two murals in the building. One was a peacock mural by a Romanian painter named Pacologue done in 1919, and on the wall of the main staircase was another painting done in 1925 by the famous Mexican artist, José Clemente Orozco. The colonial mansion was built in the late sixteenth century, in 1598 according to some accounts. It has a mixture of Arabic and Baroque influences. About 150 years after it was built, the owners had it completely covered on three sides with hand-painted blue-and-white Talavera tiles from the state of Puebla, Mexico. For my family, Puebla was a special place, as it was the birthplace of my maternal grandmother.

There are many stories surrounding the reason they covered the three sides of the house in tiles. One says that the lady of the house merely wanted to flaunt her family's immense wealth and status by using the expensive Talavera tiles. Another story claims a father was so disgusted and disappointed with his son's lack of ambition and success in life that he told him he'd never be able to build his house of tiles, meaning he'd never amount to anything. When he eventually inherited the colonial mansion from his father, he used the Talavera tiles on the house, inside and out. Who knows what the truth was, but one thing was certain, there had to be a juicy story there somewhere. The waiters were always willing to share the stories they had heard, and we heard many versions. It all added to the mystery and glamour.

Sanborns was always our special spot to meet and plan our next adventure. We'd seen the National Mexican Folkloric Dance Troupe perform at Bellas Artes the week before. We'd gone to the National Museum of Anthropology and also gone ice skating.

Carolina informed us that our next outing wouldn't be as tame. She announced that we were going to a bohemian club called La Cuevita (The Cave) on Friday night to listen to music and have our fortunes read. It was becoming the hottest club in town where all the young, hip Mexican kids were flocking. Carolina was not about to be left out. She didn't want to go with just her brother, so she invited us to join her.

She mentioned in passing that it was a bit out of the way and it would be a long bus ride, so we should dress comfortably. I wasn't sure what "a bit out of the way" meant, but we were ready for a thrilling adventure.

After finishing our visit at Casa de los Azulejos, we walked slowly back to La Alameda. Of course, we were all holding hands, talking and laughing nonstop. We crossed over to the side of the street with all the storefronts and did some window-shopping and occasionally popped into an intriguing boutique. Along the way, we debated as to who'd just had the best meal. Each one of us felt he or she had eaten the superior meal, so we were at an impasse.

Once we had flagged down a taxi to take us home, we agreed that our afternoon visit at Sanborns had been the best so far, and none of us wanted the afternoon to end.

After all the goodbye hugs had been dispensed, we concluded that Casa de los Azulejos would always be our favorite place to gather with family and friends to create memories that would last a lifetime. And we had just spent the last three hours doing that exact thing.

Hipódromo de las Américas, Mexico City

IT FELT GOOD BEING A JUNIOR IN HIGH SCHOOL, on the verge of going off to college, and feeling as though I was on the fringes of adulthood.

I spent my summer vacation as I had the year before . . . in Mexico City with my father.

His job kept him there fulltime, so Nene and I spent all major holidays with our parents in the sophisticated metropolis of Mexico City, which by the way, was absolutely no sacrifice for two teenage girls.

This day in particular began like any other day. I rolled out of bed as I had for the past couple of weeks. As always, I first took a peek out the picture window in our dining room. I never tired of looking at the vastness of humanity from the bird's-eye view of our sixth-floor apartment. After taking in the sweeping vista, I took a turn right into the kitchen.

It was usually coffee with pan dulce for breakfast, but at times we would go all out and refry some black beans and have them with *bolillos*. They are similar to French bread but much smaller, a single serving size. We would split them in half, toast them in the oven, and then spread fresh unsalted butter on top. We served the beans with the *queso ranchero* we bought at the market every other day and crumble it on top of the beans. It is a salty goat cheese, one of my favorites.

However, today I opted for a simpler fare because I was feeling lazy—plain sweet bread and a cup of strong coffee.

I took my breakfast to the dining room to join my sister who had been up for a while. As I sat down, my mom breezed through the front door. She had gone downstairs to the lobby to give the doorman all our postcards that needed to be mailed.

"Thanks, Mami," I said and blew her a bunch of air kisses.

She smiled back and gave me some too. Then she said, "Your father will be back later this morning. He wanted you girls to get dressed and be ready to go with him to the Hippodrome." She mentioned this in passing as she went into the kitchen for a cup of coffee.

I jumped up and immediately ran after her. "He wants to take us to the racetrack? Really?" I asked, looking rather surprised.

"Yes, the race track. He wants to take you girls to experience the Hippodrome."

"Don't you have to be at least twenty-one to get in, like going to a nightclub?" I asked my mom.

"No, you don't have to be twenty-one to get in. Silly girl," my mom teased.

Cool, the racetrack. I had never been to one in my life. I had a gut feeling that this was going to be a very memorable day. Lucky me!

As I sat back down at the table, I said to my sister, "Aren't you excited? I mean a real racetrack with racehorses and betting. Do you think Papi will let us place a bet? We still have some spending money left from last week. What do you say? Should we ask him?"

"Are you crazy? He doesn't want us to gamble. I mean it's okay for him to do it. He's our dad, he's an adult, he can do whatever he wants, and it's his money," she was quick to reply.

"Well, I didn't mean we should spend a lot of money. I was thinking maybe fifty pesos."

"No way," she said. And that was that.

"That's fine," I said. "But I'm still betting . . . that we're going to have fun today."

My sister cracked a grin.

We headed into the bedroom to get ready. We decided to wear our white denim skirts. I wore a yellow-and-white, thin-striped polo shirt with a navy-and-white, polka-dot cotton scarf tied loosely around my neck. I've always had a thing for scarves. My sister paired her skirt with a pink madras, short-sleeved shirt and wore her hair in a ponytail.

Though weather normally is unpredictable, afternoon rains were very predictable during the summer. We loved the afternoon rain. You could set your watch by it. When we went out, we'd take our umbrellas with us. With the first drops of rain, the street vendors would pull out sheets of plastic they would sell to people trying to keep dry. The rain did a wonderful thing. It gave the city a bath and washed the smog away, at least until the following day.

While we waited for my dad, we turned on the TV and watched *tele-novelas* (soap operas). Mexican soaps were very different from their American counterparts; facial expressions and voices were more melodramatic. That's what made them so much fun to watch. We sat there for at least a half-hour, filling our heads with nonsense, until Papi arrived.

He went in to change his clothes and freshen up a bit. As we were heading out the door, my mom gave us her traditional sign of the cross over our foreheads and told us to enjoy the afternoon and be safe.

As we drove to the Hippodrome, I realized my dad was a skilled big-city driver. Being out in that traffic was like entering a zoo where all the wild animals had escaped from their cages and were running around stark raving mad. I mentally yelled at the bus driver and the taxi driver and the driver of the red VW to stay in their lanes. Wait a minute . . . what lanes? It was frightening to see cars snaking in and out with each other . . . it was like, who's in charge? I had to close my eyes because I feared for our lives and wasn't the least bit interested in seeing which car was going to hit us. I told myself I'd rather not see it coming. And I prayed a lot. You had to. It was either pray or scream. That's how I felt when my dad was driving. I never experienced that when we rode in a taxi. Since I wasn't related to the taxi driver, I just disconnected the danger. My dad's driving though, was a different story. The danger was a little too close for comfort.

We got to the track in one piece. My dad kept us close to him because it was an incredibly large area and you could easily get lost. There was also, however remote, a chance that a person could get kidnapped. We were never out of his line of sight. We went up to the *ventanilla de apuestas*, the window where you placed bets. He made a modest bet on three horses, called a trifecta. I learned the three types of betting called trifecta, *candado*, and exacta. It seemed a bit complicated, so I focused on the racetrack's beautiful landscaping.

Scooting out of the line, with my dad's ticket in hand, we went over to the viewing box in time to see the horses start out of the gate. There was so much screaming going on with people jumping up and down in anticipation of the winner. The center area of the racetrack had swans and flamingoes that looked so peaceful in direct contrast to the horses galloping past them and the energy of all those people who had placed bets, praying that this was going to be the race that made them millionaires. Hope, fear, anxiety, and adrenaline . . . they hung thickly in the air.

The race ended, and my dad won, tripling his money that time. He took us to the area next to the betting counters where all the restaurants and bars were to see if there was something we might like to eat. Papi told us about his favorite little *taquería* and suggested we might like to try that. He guaranteed that these would be the best tasting *taquitos* (small tacos) we would ever eat.

We got in the long line that wrapped around the tables in the food court. I figured the food must be delicious to have so many people in line. We finally made it to the counter and my dad ordered ten *taquitos de puerco* (pork taquitos).

Ten sounds like a lot, but they were very small. These taquitos were made with a delicate corn tortilla, filled with seasoned shredded pork, rolled up like a little cigar, and then deep-fried till crispy golden. Some people subscribe to the philosophy that anything deep-fried is delicious. We were about to find out. We got a table close to the betting counter and began to eat the taquitos.

My dad was absolutely right when he sang their praises. I was sure the secret to the success of these taquitos was the shredded pork with a unique smoky chipotle pepper seasoning. The flavor of the rich pork, along with the crispy texture of the fried tortilla, was incredible. My dad had chosen well. So well in fact that my sister and I ate three taquitos each, and my dad had the other four.

We took our full bellies over to the electronic screen to check the race schedule. There was going to be another race starting soon, and my dad wanted to place one more bet before heading home. We got back in line with the same ticket agent, and my dad placed his bet on number seven to win.

Back we went to the viewing box, as the race had started with the horses blasting through the gates. My sister and I both kept our fingers crossed, hoping my dad would again triple his money. By the time the race was coming close to ending, it was pretty obvious that number seven would not come in first. The horse, named El Bonito, came in third.

My poor dad, I knew he was disappointed. As we were heading towards the exit, he said, "*Para que vean muchachas, por eso no se juega con el dinero. Te puedes quedar sin nada; sin dinero, sin familia. No se olviden este día.*" (So you see, girls, that is why you do not play with money. You can end up with nothing, no money, and no family. Don't ever forget this day.)

We had a sobering ride home, except for an occasional frightful scare when we thought a car might broadside us.

When we entered our apartment building, my sister and I ran up the six flights of stairs, and my dad took the elevator. We reached the sixth floor at the same moment my dad stepped out of the elevator. He shook his head with bewilderment. He told us that we were the kind of people that would rather use the stairs when there was an elevator and would rather sit on the floor when there was a sofa. This was totally true. We ran up and down six flights of stairs for the exercise. That's what fifteen- and seventeen-year-olds did. We sat on the floor rather than the sofa because we were more comfortable that way. My dad frowned on our lack of sophistication, common sense, and good manners.

My mom asked us how it had gone, and we gave her a full report. She was starting dinner and told us to go take a bath, as we'd be eating soon. All of a sudden, the food smells started to make me feel queasy, like I might be revisiting my taquitos. Everything in the room started to spin, and I ran for the bathroom.

After two and a half hours of nonstop vomiting and diarrhea, I crawled into bed. I kept having to get up because I thought I was getting sick all over again, but there was nothing left to come out. Having lost a lot of fluids, I tried drinking water, but even the tiniest sip came back up. I started to run a high fever. My mom was worried, pacing and rushing to my side every time I groaned. She kept placing cool damp cloths on my forehead. My dad had told her we had eaten pork taquitos, and my mom just about came unglued. She couldn't believe that my dad had actually let us eat pork. It is so easy to get a bad piece of pork and pick up a serious case of food poisoning. My dad and sister were fine. I happened to be the lucky one who ate a piece of bad pork. I guess I gambled eating pork at the racetrack, and I lost the bet.

As the evening wore on and it was obvious I was only getting worse, my dad called his doctor and then went to an all-night pharmacy to pick up antibiotics. My fever was 102, and it felt like my brain was being deep-fried just like those taquitos.

I had nightmares that were actually more like hallucinations due to the high fever. My poor mom kept those cold wet towels on me to try to bring down the fever. Worse yet was my dad, who was just beside himself. He felt so culpable that it hurt me to see his suffering.

When it was apparent my fever was not going down, my mom told my dad that it wasn't about the pork after all. She got up quickly from my bed and did the only other thing she knew she could do. She ran to the kitchen, cracked a fresh egg into a white porcelain bowl, ran back to my room, placed it on the floor, and then slid the bowl under the bed directly under my head. She diagnosed that it wasn't food poisoning after all.

I was this ill because someone at the racetrack had given me "*el ojo*" (the evil eye). No joke, that was what she said.

By morning my fever had broken, and I was out of the woods. As the first light came into my bedroom from the large east-facing window, I opened up my eyes and asked, "What happened?" Though I was still in a very weak state, I felt a million times better than I had the night before. Everyone told me that I kept crying out, shaking like I was freezing, and tossing and turning all through the night.

My mom reached under the bed and pulled out the bowl with the raw egg she had placed there the night before. However, the egg was no longer raw. It was completely cooked through. It looked like an over-cooked hard-poached egg. All our jaws fell wide open, including my dad's, who was always skeptical about everything and always tried to be the voice of reason.

But what his voice of reason and skepticism could not dismiss were the facts that my fever had gone just as mysteriously as it had appeared and that the egg my mom had placed under my bed had been completely cooked by the force of my body fighting off the evil eye, or so the theory goes.

As my mind began to clear, I thought about everything that had happened the day before. I realized two things:

First, my gut feeling had been accurate. The day at the racetrack with my sister and dad had been a most memorable day . . . and night.

Second, my dad had also been accurate when he said, "Don't ever forget this day," because I never have.

Les Amis

IF YOU'VE EVER HAD A MOMENT in your life when you felt like all the planets were aligned, like all was well with the world, like you were the happiest you'd ever been in your entire life, like it couldn't get better than this moment . . . then you know exactly what I am talking about.

I've had great moments in my life, real Kodak moments like everyone else. However, the weekend I spent with my mom when she hitched a ride with my roommate's parents all the way to Austin . . . just to see me . . . just for the heck of it . . . just to spend one autumn weekend with me, well, I'd have to say that was nothing short of nirvana.

I was in my junior year at the University of Texas. It was early November of 1972. I remember that because of the weather and how it made me feel. Austin can get pretty hot, but the best of times were the autumn and winter months when we had a break from the heat. The temperature was perfect . . . really chilly to cold but not freezing-Alaska kind of cold, just bundle-up kind of cold or wear-your-boots kind of cold. That meant it was early November and giving us a hint of what December might bring.

Financially, I was barely squeaking by. I had no spare cash to go back home to see my parents during any of the normal breaks between semesters. I felt somewhat stranded. So you can imagine travel during my university years was not much of an option.

One of my roommate's parents contacted my mom and told her there was room in their car for one more person and offered to bring her up to see me if she'd like to come along. I'm sure my mom wasted no time in accepting the ride. That's how her arrival in Austin during a glorious autumn weekend came about.

It was a long drive from Brownsville to Austin, at least a good six hours. To get through the King Ranch was an achievement in itself. It was a privately owned ranch of 825,000 acres. I wondered if my mom had spotted any javelina, coyotes, deer, Rio Grande turkeys, feral hogs, or armadillos. There was an abundance of wildlife throughout the South Texas ranch land but nothing like the abundance of wild life on my college campus that, incidentally, my mom would witness firsthand.

My mom and Gracie's parents arrived on a Thursday evening just before supper. When I saw her walk through the front door of our apartment, I was overwhelmed with emotion. It was not until that moment that I began to realize how homesick I was and, in particular, how much I missed my mom. Gracie decided to stay with her parents at their hotel room downtown, freeing up her bed for my mom. It was so much nicer having my mom stay with me, rather than in a hotel.

Our dinner was quick and easy that night—grilled cheese sandwiches on French bread with a cup of canned tomato soup. We didn't want to waste any precious time together.

I told my mom all about the classes I was taking, which subjects were most interesting, and new friends and classmates. I finally stopped talking when I realized that my mom had fallen asleep. It was only 9:00 p.m., but I was sure the trip had been tiring. I put an extra blanket on top of her covers in case she got cold during the night.

We both woke up early the following morning when my alarm clock went off at seven o'clock. That gave us plenty of time to get dressed and walk to campus. I took a quick peek out the front door to check the temperature outside, and the thermometer read 56 degrees, perfect.

I suggested to my mom she wear her beige wool pantsuit with her black turtleneck sweater and floral-print silk scarf. I remember thinking about how beautiful she looked that day, like she had just walked off a New York fashion runway. I didn't realize until now that my mom was only fifty-two at the time. She was still so young and in her prime with much more living to do.

My style was more bohemian. I threw on a teal-colored, lightweight sweater, a green paisley scarf, tied loosely around my neck, and my favorite double-breasted green tweed jacket. My fitted Levi's were tucked neatly into the caramel-colored leather boots I'd gotten years ago on one of our trips to Mexico City. In honor of my mom's visit, I topped off my outfit with the merlot-colored wool cap she had knitted for me before I left for Austin.

We began our walk to campus, which was a one-mile trek through a park-like neighborhood. The wind was sharp and invigorating. You could feel the air fill your lungs and just imagine the oxygen-rich blood circulating throughout your body. What a great feeling that was . . . very alive and present in the moment.

Because we were so animated in our conversation, we had

naturally taken a speed-walking pace and reached campus faster than I ever had before. There was enough time for us to catch a tasty and very cheap breakfast at the Student Union.

There, I took my mom through my regular routine. I always grabbed the campus newspaper, the *Daily Texan*, picked up a tray for food, and got in line. I poured myself a large glass of orange juice, a cup of black coffee, one homemade buttermilk biscuit drowning in white gravy, and one sausage patty. That was it. My mom served herself the same thing. We ate our breakfast at a leisurely pace, as I still had an hour before class.

Today being Friday meant that it was one of the lighter days on my schedule. After breakfast, we walked to my 9:30 sociology class. It must have been pretty uneventful because I can't remember too many details. Or the reason I may not remember is that my 11:00 class eclipsed it.

At the time, Art, Modern Literature and Media in the 20th Century was an unconventional class. It had been wildly popular, along with the bearded, longhaired professor, during the late 1960s. The class was still considered avant-garde and innovative.

In this particular class, we not only read contemporary literature but also studied modern art and film as it related to the literature. We explored movements such as Dadaism, surrealism, modern art, and abstract art. We went to a university screening room to watch films chosen for us by our professor. And our novels were fairly contemporary.

The class was held in a large auditorium that could hold at least four hundred students. The professor stood mysteriously in the back, not very visible to most students, and spoke through a microphone. As he began his lecture, he projected images on multiple screens that circled half of the auditorium. These were very large, about a third the size of a theatre screen. There were constant visual images flashing before you with music in the background. My mom commented on the fact that the professor was nowhere to be seen. Wasn't he supposed to stand up front, at a podium and visible to all his students?

On this particular day, our professor lectured on erotica in art, literature, and film. If my mom was disturbed by not seeing my professor standing in front of the class, I couldn't help but wonder what might happen next.

His instruction began as erotic paintings of people doing all sorts of things . . . images of nudes in an array of postures began flashing all over the screens. He had samples of shock art and porn. This went on for an hour and a half. My mom was bombarded with larger-than-life erotic images in every size, shape, and color. To tie it all together, the professor read excerpts from novels containing lots of swearing, vulgar language, and graphic imagery. That was the type of novel we were currently studying. The lecture hammered away loudly over the heavy metal music jarring every nerve in my mom's gentle psyche.

Amid all the chaos around us, my mom appeared to remain very calm and composed, all the while keeping her eyes glued to the screens and the flashing images.

When our lecture was over, we walked out of the auditorium. I waited for her to say something, but she just smiled.

I suggested we find a nice place to have a late lunch. We headed towards The Drag, which was a nickname given to Guadalupe Street, which fronted the university. It had the campus bookstore, some small restaurants, a few boutiques, and various gift shops.

On weekends, hippies and artists threw down big blankets on the sidewalk and sold their wares—lots of handmade jewelry, leather goods, clothing, tie-dyed T-shirts, candles, and other crafts. The atmosphere was always lively on The Drag. You'd have colorful musicians strumming guitars or playing fiddles or the Janis Joplin wannabes singing their hearts out. It was a pivotal moment in history that flashed by way too quickly, like a haunting dream that was over before you knew it began. Fortunately, some of those great days became memories.

My mom took my hand, and we ran across the street holding hands like a couple of girlfriends and started to laugh.

My mom looked at me and said, "Honey, I am so glad that I got a chance to come see you and live a day of your life with you."

"I'm glad too," I said and gave her a big hug right there on The Drag. "What about that lecture? Did it upset you?"

My mom grinned and said, "It didn't bother me that much. Really. I understand that times have changed. The world you live in is not the world I grew up in. That's okay. Things change, sometimes for the better, sometimes not." She winked. "I'm fine. How else can I be on such a beautiful day, spending it with my daughter?"

And she meant ever word she said. I knew the content of that class didn't bother her because she was in the moment with me, not with the class. My mom loved everything about the day because it was part of me, of what I was living. She felt content and so did I.

As we strolled along The Drag, holding hands, we looked into shop windows and oohed and aahed at all the lovely things in their showcases. The day was still perfect with a chill in the air, crisp and clean. I felt warm and cozy with my mom next to me. It even sounded as though the clunking of my boots and the clicking of my mom's heels were in sync with their own special harmony.

We rounded the corner, and the wind blew through my

long, straight, shoulder-length hair. On the side street was a café called Les Amis (The Friends). Very popular with the university crowd, it had the atmosphere of a French café with outdoor seating close to the sidewalk. The indoor seating had a fireplace that was lit when the weather became cool. Today, most of the patrons were sitting inside, close to the warmth of the fire.

MY MOM WITH ME ON A TRIP TO ACAPULCO, MEXICO, THE SUMMER OF 1970, BEFORE I STARTED COLLEGE.

We joined them at a table near the fireplace. The flames were a golden glowing red-hot haven of warmth and comfort. My mom quickly picked up a menu and began to look at the food choices. She said right away, "Oh, I know exactly what we need." Just then the waiter came up and asked if he could bring us a drink or an appetizer.

My mom promptly said, "We'll both have a glass of red wine, please, and an order of savory crêpes."

And without skipping a beat, I went from being a little kid who missed her mommy to being a woman who was best friends with her mom. My mom had just offered me a new role in her life . . . and with that, our mother/daughter relationship had shifted and my life had changed forever.

As we sat there sipping our wine, I realized that I had never seen my mom pick up a glass of wine, much less any other type of alcohol, in my entire life, ever.

We lingered in the café, enjoying our crêpes and wine by the toasty fireplace. And every time my mom had a flashback to my English class, she would laugh, shake her head in dismay, and take another sip of wine. Since we were almost finished with our meal, she decided to order us another glass of wine and asked for the dessert menu.

As the afternoon unfolded into early evening, we were treated to one of those rare delayed sunsets where everything turns a warm shade of golden orange and glows for a long time. It was magical. My life felt like it was in perfect harmony with nature.

Neither one of us was in a rush to be anywhere other than where we were at that moment, by the warm fire at Les Amis, savoring our wine and dessert, as best friends most likely would.

Our afternoon had mysteriously vanished, along with our wine, and it was time to say goodbye to Les Amis.

When we stepped outside, we were greeted by a cold wind swirling about, which created mischief with my mom's scarf and my long brown hair. We called a cab to take us back to my apartment.

And as we stood there, arm in arm, on the corner of Les Amis and The Drag, waiting for our cab to arrive, my mom and I both let out a deep and delightful sigh of contentment.

Simple Pleasures

WHEN YOU'RE A LITTLE KID, every second of every day is an adventure and therefore special. Or at least it was like that for me. I remember wanting to remain a kid for as long as possible. The thought of growing up was not overly appealing to me. I relished my youth and my freedom. I think there was a part of me that knew the feeling of freedom would be fleeting.

But for the time being, it would be years before I had to pay my dues. I was only seven years old and had just finished the first grade. My sister and I had come to spend part of the summer with Bueli and Tía Lolis in Nuevo Laredo.

It was July, and the official hot season was just around the corner, usually in full swing by early August. Nuevo Laredo had what was called *la canícula*, which was similar to opening furnace doors and letting out all the raging heat into the neighborhood. This intense heat wave lasted for many weeks. I remember thinking that la canícula surely made Nuevo Laredo hotter than Hell, though I had no desire to verify it.

The heat was merely an observation of how things felt at the moment. It never stopped me from doing anything I wanted to do. The heat never kept me indoors. It never kept me from running around and playing outside until I'd collapse with heat exhaustion. Nope, it never stopped me from having fun.

Simple pleasures were what we experienced daily, never anything expensive, fancy, or store-bought. As I grew older and life took its toll on my heart, I was always able to dig through my countless memories and tap into my many happy places. Places infused with unconditional love, like the kind I felt when I stayed with Bueli and Tía Lolis.

We'd been visiting for a few weeks and had our daily routine. After getting out of our pj's, we'd wash our faces and put on play clothes, usually shorts with elastic bands and sleeveless cotton shirts. My sister and I had the job of setting the table for breakfast. I loved doing that because we got to unlock the *vitrina* (china cabinet). It was not fancy, but it was beautiful, nonetheless. It was painted glossy white and had red plastic handles on the glass-paneled doors. The shelves were lined with plastic cloth that had colorful pictures of fruits like cherries, bananas, and pineapples.

Inside the cabinet were all types of china. They were a bit mismatched, but that was the allure. You always got to try a different plate or bowl. They all had different colored flowers along the scalloped borders or in the centers or in both places. They looked old and well-worn with the crackled glazes. I loved how they looked, so decorative. Our plates at home were much plainer and all matched. I liked my granny's better.

This morning in particular, Tía Lolis gave us a choice of scrambled eggs and flour tortillas or pan dulce and her special sweetened gorditas. My sister and I both voted in unison,

"*Pan dulce y gorditas, por favor.*" (Sweet bread and gorditas, please.) Her gorditas were a cross between a gordita and a flour tortilla. They were small, maybe three-inch rounds, similar to a gordita. However, a regular gordita would be made with *masa harina* (corn flour) and lard, but hers were made with white flour. And they were much thicker than a regular flour tortilla. She also added shortening and sugar to make them sweet, like a pastry. After she cooked them on a *comal* (cast-iron griddle), she'd fill a large glass jar to the top and let us have them for snacks. We took out small plates and cups with saucers for our coffee. It made us feel like big girls to drink coffee, though it was really hot milk with a drop of coffee.

The milk was fresh and non-pasteurized, so my granny needed to boil it first. We stood by the stove and fought over who'd get to skim the *nata* (skin) that formed on top as it boiled. We both liked scooping it out and eating the buttery nata with a spoon. One spoonful was about all you got after boiling the milk, so it was a treat.

Our day was spent like most of the days there, outdoors. We went to the backyard and explored all the fruit trees to scavenge for fruit that may already have fallen to the ground. No luck. It was clean. It looked like Bueli had already been there. She liked to sweep under the trees and then water down the dirt and give her trees a long drink early in the morning before it got too hot.

In the far back of the yard was an old, somewhat spooky-looking storage shed. Since we weren't doing anything else, Nene and I went in to explore. In the bowels of the shed were lots of old photos, clothes, and broken equipment that needed repair. It was like going into a pirate's lair and stumbling upon hidden treasures, such as mirrors, lamps, ladies' hats, a bowl of keys, shoes, boxes that were sealed, and bulging

suitcases that were scattered about. There were a couple of broken birdcages, some rusted metal planters, army cots, and an
assortment of tools. No telling what kind of treasures lay bur-
ied underneath all the layers. The hot, stale air in the shed was
suffocating. Our only recourse was to go back outside into the
fresh air and the sizzling afternoon sun.

As we walked around the yard, we discovered one of my
granny's fig trees loaded and drooping with the weight of the
ripe figs. Nene and I looked at each other and agreed there
was only one thing we could do—climb the tree. I couldn't
reach the lowest limb, so I stepped up onto Nene's knees and
then stood on her shoulders, grabbed a limb, and hoisted
myself up. I was only seven, but I'd already climbed a tree or
two back home with my friend, Chucky. I knew what I was
doing. I was a seasoned tree climber.

This was a 'Black Mission' fig tree, one of my granny's
prized trees. She enjoyed serving fresh chilled figs with a
hunk of Mexican cheese. Tía Lolis preferred making homemade cookies that were like Fig Newtons only better because
she made her filling from scratch.

I grabbed the fattest, juiciest-looking fig I could reach and
claimed the first one for myself. It had a teardrop shape with
a thin black velvety skin. When I pulled it apart, the fruit
inside was a rich deep ruby, and it tasted sweeter than honey.
As my eyes rolled around in my head and my senses took in
all the smells and flavors of the sweet fig, I heard Nene yelling, "Paty, hurry up and throw me down a fig. You're taking
too long. Bueli is going to find us and get mad. Hurry." I
thought, get mad? Why would she get mad?

I tossed a fat fig down to Nene, who had cupped her
hands like a basket. "Bull's-eye," I yelled gleefully. I was ready
for a second one and reached out to the limb that was in
full sun. That fig looked extra-large. "Hey, Nene, your eyes

are going to pop out when you see how huge this one is." I plucked it from the limb and tossed it to my lookout as her reward. Feeling so accomplished, I let out a victory laugh. "These are so good. Aren't we lucky?"

It was my turn for the next sweet black beauty. I turned around, and behind me was a branch loaded with at least two dozen figs. I couldn't believe that the birds hadn't gotten to these figs first. However, I could see another bunch that had been pecked at by the birds. Hmm. I wondered how my granny was able keep them away. Off went the next fig. "This one's mine, Nene. You'll have to wait a minute while I enjoy it."

I took my time looking at the fig, holding it up to my nose, and sniffing deeply. I was intrigued by how great it smelled and, after I took a bite, also by how great it tasted. Figs were lucky being so beautiful, I thought. Once again, my sister broke my transcendental moment.

"Paty," she yelled, "you'd better get down from the tree, NOW. I heard the kitchen door slam, and I think Bueli is coming. We're going to get in trouble. Come on . . . climb down on to my shoulders," she shrieked.

"Okay, but I don't think we'll get in trouble. We didn't do anything wrong. We're supposed to eat lots of fruit while we're here, remember?" And no sooner did those words come out of my fig-scented mouth than I caught sight of Bueli coming around the lime tree with a broom in her hand, waving it around.

"*Paty, bájate, ahorita mismo . . . ,*" my granny scolded as she neared the tree. She had just told me to get down, immediately, all the while waving her broom around like she was trying to scare us. She got up to the tree wielding her broom and brushed at my legs, motioning me down.

I quickly stepped onto Nene's shoulders and jumped off.

Bueli threw down her broom and mumbled under her breath, "*Ay que muchachitas tan traviesas.*" (Oh, you little girls are so mischievous.) And then she started to laugh.

Just then some crows started to land on the figs, and Bueli picked up her broom and commenced swinging. Birds started going off in all directions. They looked pretty funny. The birds squawked loudly and flew off a bit, then circled around and tried to dive-bomb the figs, cawing like they were trying to scare us off.

Bueli started shooting idle threats at the birds, "*Lárguense de aquí, pájaros feos, lárguense. . . . Quítense de los higos ahora mismo o los voy a pescar y asarlos con chiles. . . . Regrésense al otro lado del Rio Grande.*" (Get out of here, you ugly birds, get out. . . . Get off those figs immediately or else I'll catch you and throw you in the oven to bake with some chilies. . . . Go back to the other side of the Rio Grande.)

Bueli told Nene to run back to the house and grab two more brooms that were out by the bathhouse. Seconds later, Nene was back with the brooms. Then Bueli yelled at us to swing the brooms around to scare off the birds. All the while we did this, my granny continued to come up with some pretty creative threats against the birds, hoping, somehow, they would understand her words.

We swung our brooms around and made loud noises for the next fifteen minutes, until the last bird had flown away, heading due south. My granny gave us a satisfied grin, placed her hands on her wide hips, and said, "*Ándale pues.*" (All right then.)

She sent Nene and me back to the house and had us bring out three small, red wicker fruit baskets that were hanging on a yellow hook by the back screen door. As Bueli picked the ripe figs within her reach, she handed them to us one by one, and we placed them gingerly in the baskets until they were all full. Once all the ripe figs had been picked, she wiped her sweaty face on her floral-print, cotton apron and told us we'd be tasting these tonight with supper and my aunt would be making us a special batch of her fig bars.

As we walked back to the house, Bueli told us she'd been protecting the figs just for us and it had been a challenge at times but was glad our teamwork had prevailed as we saved most of the figs. She looked so proud, and I felt so loved.

Bueli never scolded me for climbing the tree. I thought that was pretty cool. And she didn't get mad at us for eating the figs either. I knew she wouldn't.

The following day, when we were playing in the backyard, I noticed that Bueli had left a ladder propped up against the fig tree. Oh, and two little red wicker fruit baskets.

Let Them Eat Cake!

I‌T WAS THE DAY BEFORE MY EIGHTH BIRTHDAY. No one had said anything at all about celebrating.

My mom and dad had driven my sister and me up to Nuevo Laredo on a Saturday several weeks earlier for our traditional summer vacation at my granny's house. Then they headed back home to Brownsville the following day. I began to wonder if anyone knew it was going to be my birthday. What troubled me was Mom wasn't there to make sure I got a birthday cake. Would anyone else remember? Had she left instructions for someone else?

It wasn't like I wanted a party or anything like that. We never had a big birthday party. We really didn't care. What we wanted, though, was to get a delicious birthday cake. That was more than enough.

I suppose I could have asked my aunt about it, but somehow that didn't feel right. A person shouldn't ask about a sensitive subject like that, at least that's what I thought.

Instead, I opted to worry about it and stew over it all that day and into the next day.

My parents had not stayed longer with us as my dad never got time off from work. He was employed by one of the largest banks in Mexico and worked directly for one of the owners. This family was well-known throughout Mexico because they owned so many banks. Even back then, they were known to be multi-millionaires. It never seemed fair to me that my father would work so hard with no time off, other than half a day on Saturday and all day Sunday. No vacation time that I can remember during my entire childhood, ever.

Funny thing was every summer we'd go play with the banker's daughters who were around our ages. My dad's boss would send his black Lincoln Mark V limousine to pick us up at my granny's and drive us to his house, which was a secluded mansion on a private estate. When you reached it, you'd drive through these enormous flamboyant gates and up a winding driveway to the mansion. I actually got lost in the house once while we were playing hide and seek. It was so massive that finding me on the same day I got lost was nothing short of a miracle.

The banker's daughters may have been very wealthy, but they didn't have anyone to play with. My sister and I were just the opposite. Our family may not have had much money, but we never lacked for love, attention, affection, companionship, or friendship. We were definitely the millionaires, I thought.

The girls had a separate room that was their very own playroom. Mind you, that room was probably bigger than my granny's entire house. It had a closet about the size of Granny's living room filled with play clothes—all kinds of dress-up clothes, like evening gowns worn only once by their mom and real costumes for clowns, Arabian Nights characters, cowboys/cowgirls, Indians, belly-dancers, pirates, and more. The choices were endless in that big old closet. Then there were all the extras, such as costume jewelry from a Kress five-and-dime store, hats, shoes, and makeup. Stored in a Louis XIV armoire were board games, decks of cards, books, and jacks. On the daybed, the stuffed toys were all neatly arranged by species. The only thing you needed that you couldn't buy at a store was imagination.

It was a bit overwhelming for a little kid like me to walk into a playroom that resembled a department store.

I'll never forget the first time I saw their playroom. It just didn't look real. I mean, what parent buys all this stuff for their kids? What ever happened to playing with your regular clothes and using your imagination? That's what we always did. When we played at our house, a knight's sword wasn't a sword at all; it was a stick. The reins for the horse weren't reins; they were my long braids that hung down to my waist, and you guessed it, I was also the horse.

If the house-size playroom wasn't enough to intimidate you, there were always the Olympic-size swimming pool in the backyard, the four-car garage to the side of the main mansion, and the servants' quarters that looked like a two-story apartment building. The mansion was staffed with an army of servants, including maids, housecleaners, cooks, nannies, gardeners, chauffeurs, and tutors. I suppose my sister and I, the playmates from the barrio, were considered essential personnel.

That morning, the day before my birthday, I was surprised to see the limo arrive. It was its first visit to my granny's house since Nene and I had arrived that summer. I didn't know we were going over to play. However, it was crazy hot, and their whole mansion was air-conditioned, so it seemed like a pretty good tradeoff. Underneath my smile was a frown that feared no one would remember my birthday.

My aunt was comfortable letting us play with the banker's daughters because he was her boss too. She was a clerk at his bank in Nuevo Laredo.

Try to imagine how this must have looked to a nosy neighbor who could have been watching. A big black limo drives into this very poor neighborhood, what most people would call a barrio. On the side street to my granny's house was an old neighborhood cantina. Not a fancy bar or martini bar like they have now. It was the kind of cantina that would have barroom brawls and drunks crawling in and out at all hours.

This bar looked like it had been plucked right out of a Hollywood movie set. It had double, swinging half-doors, just like in those old westerns, the creaky wood floors, and the bar against the wall that faced the doors. It always had customers. I know this because Bueli's house backed up to this cantina and you could hear the noise. Every time we walked down the street to the *raspa* (shaved ice) stand or walked to the bus stop, we would pass in front of the bar. When the doors swung open, I always peeked in. I couldn't help myself.

It was filled with loud men, drinking, smoking, and banging their glasses on the bar for another round. Above the bar was an ornate, gold-framed, horizontal mirror, and on each side of the mirror was a painting of a reclining nude; the bar was pretty much the old stereotype of a western bar.

When we slept outside on a hot night, you could hear the noise from the bar, and to be perfectly honest, there were times I'd lie awake for a long time, afraid of the drunken noises from next door, until exhaustion finally won and I'd close my eyes. The noise didn't seem to bother my aunt, granny, or sister. Only me.

On the day before my birthday, the limo drove through Bueli's neighborhood, passed the local cantina, turned right at the corner, and pulled up to her humble home. A chauffeur with a starched black uniform, black cap, and white gloves stepped out. He went around to the passenger side and opened the backseat door. Evidently, the girls, Lucy and Sally, hadn't come along for the ride. It was only the chauffeur. Nene and I climbed aboard the limo express, and the chauffeur shut the heavy doors, making a soft thump as they closed. The windows had a dark tint, so we couldn't be seen from the outside, but of course we could see out. And as we drove away, we waved to my aunt, but she couldn't see us through the tinted glass.

As we passed through the enormous wrought-iron gates up the winding driveway to the house, we started to get excited since this was the first time we'd been to see the girls since our arrival. They had just gotten in from visiting their own grandmother in Mexico City.

The chauffeur helped us out of the car and escorted us into the house where the head servant was waiting for us. She took us up the winding staircase to the second-floor playroom where the girls were waiting. They had already started pulling out some of the clothes from the closet. When they saw us come in, they dropped everything on the floor and came running up and gave us both hugs and kisses.

They both looked like life-size dolls in dotted-Swiss, ruffled dresses. Sally's dress was lavender with a purple ribbon around the waist, making her look like a jewel with her red curly hair and freckles. Lucy's light-green dress with a forest-green ribbon looked stunning with her black hair, porcelain-white skin, and emerald-colored eyes. They told us how lonely they'd been this summer. They had been at their grandmother's all of June and didn't get to go anywhere because she'd been ill. All their cousins were much older, so they had no one their own age to play with. So there we were . . .

Ten costume changes later, the servant came up to tell us that lunch was ready. Lucy said we wanted to eat upstairs, so the servants very obligingly brought us our lunch. What a difference in menu from my granny's house. We had tuna sandwiches on white bread with no crust, cucumber slices, thick tomato wedges, and slices of cantaloupe and mangos. I enjoyed the mangos the most; they were so sweet and juicy. What seemed weird, though, was that the mangos had been sliced into bite size pieces. You ate your mango with a fork. At my granny's we got the whole mango, which was chilled, and that was it. You got to peel it and eat it right off the seed, like a Popsicle. We always made a mess while eating our mangos, so she'd have us sit outside on the porch. We'd have juice all over our arms and legs and the concrete floor by the time we had finished. Bueli would turn on the garden hose and wash us down right there on the spot. We loved that as much as eating the mango. That would give us a quick cooling down, and because it was so hot, our clothes would be dry within minutes.

The day at the mansion flew by. We played Old Maid, Candy Land, dominos, puppets, and lots of dress up. My personal favorite was my rendition of a cowgirl with a rhinestone tiara, a long strand of pearls, white opera gloves, and the essential cowboy boots. My sister's favorite was her unique take on a kimono with high-tops and a top hat. Sally went straight for the princess ballerina look with a lavender tutu, sparkly slippers, and a small queen's crown. Lucy had on her mom's white-linen, three-piece suit and added a briefcase and a pair of red glasses. She turned into an *abogada* (attorney).

At 5:00 p.m. the servant came upstairs to tell us the chauffeur was waiting to take Nene and me home. The girls wanted us to spend the night, but I really wanted to go back to my granny's. I wanted to be home on my birthday. I thought it would've been nice to know if my aunt had made any party plans so I could've invited the girls. Since it seemed nothing was planned, I didn't bring it up.

Lucy and Sally had said they'd see us again real soon. We waved goodbye from inside the monster limo, even though we knew they couldn't see in the window.

Nene and I got home and told Bueli and Tía all about our day, the mansion, what we ate, all the play clothes, and the swimming pool. We left nothing out. I told Tía that even though I had had lots of fun, I always had more fun with her and Bueli and I'd rather stay with them. She assured me that was fine. Tía felt like the girls would've had more fun playing with us at our house, so she said maybe next time they could visit us instead; she'd talk to her boss tomorrow.

I was left wondering if anything birthday related was going to happen tomorrow. My aunt gave no clues about it being someone's birthday. I couldn't even bring myself to ask my sister if she had heard anything, so I stewed some more.

Oh well . . .

Tired from worry, I went to bed and finally fell asleep.

That night we had a bit of a reprieve from the intense heat. My aunt set up cots on the side porch and said it was a good night for sleeping outdoors. It was going to cool off very quickly, and it would feel like we were sleeping in a nice cold air-conditioned room, so she left us a lightweight blanket in case it got too chilly. She was right because sometime during the night I found myself groping around for the blanket. Nuevo Laredo had that desert type of climate that could go from blazing hot to very chilly in the same day.

In the morning, the temperature was so perfect under the covers that, even though I heard my granny and aunt get up, I had no desire to disturb my covers or my semi-sleeping state. You know what a great feeling that is—to have reached the perfect temperature of cozy but not at too warm in sheets cool but not icy cold. You don't ever want to have to move or wake up from that moment of bliss. That was how I felt on my birthday morning. In fact, I had forgotten about it being my birthday, even after all the obsessing I had done the day before.

As I let out a sigh of rapture with the covers all the way over my head and thinking, "I'm not moving from this spot, even if there is a loud barroom brawl next door or if I hear police sirens or even gunshots. I'm not moving an inch."

Just then, I heard my granny, aunt, and sister coming up singing, "*Estas son las mañanitas que cantaba el Rey David, a las muchachas bonitas se las cantaba así . . . ,*" The traditional Mexican happy birthday song. They hadn't forgotten it was my birthday.

After all the singing and hugging woke me up, Bueli said I could choose a breakfast menu. Whatever I wanted. And I could decide if we ate indoors or out on the porch. I thought that was pretty special. I chose breakfast al fresco and my favorite food of all time—refried black beans, homemade flour tortillas with butter and Ranchero cheese. That combination can still make me a happy woman any day, anytime, anywhere.

Since it was my birthday, Tía said I didn't have to do the dishes and that she'd take my place and help my sister. She had me go take a bath and get ready for the day.

This time I decided I was going to fill up my own Olympic bathtub and soak until I resembled a prune. I took a leisurely bath, singing in the tub, washing my hair, and splashing around, making a general mess of things.

I finally forced myself to get out of the tub and get dressed. My aunt had laid out my clothes for me, a white cotton T-shirt with pink shorts. I always felt my aunt wanted us to look nice. Their motto was always something like, "Even if you only have one dress to wear, it should always be clean and well-pressed. Being poor doesn't mean you can't look nice." Something might have gotten lost in the translation, but I knew we always looked nice.

After Nene had her chance to bathe and get dressed, she came out to the porch and found me stretched out in the hammock that was off to one side of the front porch. There was a string nailed to the side of the house that you grabbed onto and pulled if you wanted the hammock to swing. "Nene, do you want to jump on?" I asked.

She instantly said, "No, I'd rather get on slowly, one leg at a time if you don't mind."

"Well, since today is my birthday, I get to have whatever I want; I want you to climb up on the hammock any way you want," I said.

There we stayed, slowly rocking the hammock and letting life go on by without us. It felt so good.

Bueli had some of her birdcages on the side of the porch, so every time I swung the hammock, I could see the canaries at eye level. They were so delicate and had such a beautiful song. The fact that my granny took such good care of her little birds made me feel very proud of her. She would watch over the little bird eggs to make sure each canary would hatch. Some colorful parakeets she loved were outside by her bedroom window. Bueli would go shopping at the Mercado (farmer's market) for specialty items for her birds and come home with dried chili pepper seeds, dried ants, flies, mosquitoes, bug larvae, and other assorted dried bugs for them to nibble on, in addition to the special birdseed she bought. My granny said it made her canaries sing more beautifully and gave her parakeets brighter colors on their feathers.

My birthday morning breezed on by while Nene and I swung away on the hammock.

As if by magic, the black limo pulled up in the front of our house. Out popped the chauffeur, and he quickly moved to the passenger side, opening those heavy doors. Who should appear from the bowels of the limo but Sally and Lucy . . . and they were bearing gifts. I was absolutely surprised.

Because I was caught so off-guard, I nearly rolled us right off the hammock, coming dangerously close to knocking over the yellow wooden birdcage with the precious singing canaries. As I overcompensated by swinging the hammock in the other direction, I rolled Nene and me completely over, and we both landed on the concrete floor, face down. Though it felt like we'd been hit over the head with a bag of bricks, I told my sister, "Better us than Granny's canaries." She got up holding onto her nose and head and simply bobbed her head in agreement.

As I hobbled up to the gate, my aunt came out of the house to greet the girls and talk with the chauffeur. They agreed on the time he'd return for Sally and Lucy.

My aunt greeted the girls, grabbed my hand, and said, "*Vámonos muchachitas, al jardín.*" (Come on, little girls, to the garden.) Then Tía Lolis, wearing a yellow, floral, short-sleeved dress with a white embroidered apron, led the way to the backyard while we trailed behind her like little newborn chicks. What a sight.

As we swung around the corner, I saw a card table set up at one end of the patio. On the far wall there was a pin-the-tail-on-the-donkey sheet. Strung all around the patio were festive party lights. *Papel picado* (cut-out paper) banners (a traditional Mexican paper art form) said "*Feliz Cumpleaños*" (Happy Birthday). There was a huge piñata shaped like a donkey hanging in the center of the patio. Standing underneath the piñata was my granny in her signature "hands on her hips" stance and a huge smile across her face.

Everyone sang a round of "Las Mañanitas" (a happy birthday song; literally "little mornings"). I just stood there frozen with my mouth wide open, looking at the piñata.

Tía Lolis and Bueli had secretly planned my birthday party without a hitch, just like a seasoned pair of secret agents. They were good.

We all took a turn at pinning the tail on the donkey, while my aunt brought out refreshments. She had made one of my favorite drinks, a *agua de tamarindo* (tamarind drink) plus gorditas with beans and cheese, shredded lettuce, and chopped tomato. The next event was breaking the piñata. It's a Mexican tradition that whenever there is a birthday, wedding, cultural or religious holiday, or La Posada, the holiday celebrations leading up to Christmas, you always have piñatas.

We each had turns hitting the piñata with a broomstick. The protocol for playing this game is that first you get blindfolded, are spun around so you're not sure in which direction you're facing and a bit dizzy, and then start swinging away. Of course, all the while my granny maneuvered the rope from which the donkey was suspended. She would either drop it closer to our broomstick or raise it up higher so we'd miss it. Everyone yelled out confusing advice, "Hit it higher, now lower, now to your right side, now higher." Eventually everyone got in a few good smacks, and so the piñata began to break open and all sorts of treats trickled out until the final big WHACK and it broke completely open, and all the candy, peanuts, oranges, and pieces of sugar cane fell out. That's when pandemonium kicked in as we ran to scoop up the loot. Good fun.

And if this wasn't enough glory for one child to have on her birthday, Tía made sure that I would have one more treat before the day was over.

As the kitchen door slammed, everyone began to sing "Happy birthday," and my aunt appeared with the biggest birthday cake I'd ever seen. It was a four-layer coconut cake with white meringue icing, sprinkled with toasted coconut, all made from scratch. Each layer had homemade guava filling and icing.

I ran up and gazed at the masterpiece. I asked my aunt, "*¿Para mi, Tía?*" (Is this for me, Tía?)

Tía answered, "*Pues mi Patita claro que si.*" (Well my, little Paty, of course.) She set the cake on the table and then gave me a birthday hug.

The cake was so tall that the only way I could blow out the candles on its top was to stand on my chair. I closed my eyes, made a wish, and blew out all the candles as everyone stood by clapping.

Tía Lolis told us we could eat as much cake as we wanted. So we did. That was the most delicious cake any of us had ever tasted. After we all had finished our first piece, I opened presents.

According to Benito, the chauffeur, Sally and Lucy had made a special trip across the border into Laredo to a Kress five-and-dime store to buy presents earlier that morning. Lucy had picked out a beautiful rhinestone tiara that was even more elaborate than her own. She told me she liked it more than her own tiara, so that's why she bought it; it was special. Sally had chosen a pair of red-and-turquoise leather cowboy boots that were a little big so I could grow into them. Nene had made me an apron just like my aunt's because she knew how much I admired it. She had apparently been working on it whenever I took a nap or went out to the Mercado with my granny. I had wondered why she never tagged along.

After all the presents were opened, we ate more cake and

packed some cake for the girls to take home. Their chauffeur arrived at 5:00 p.m. to pick them up.

I gave everyone a big hug, including Benito, and thanked them for helping make my birthday so special.

As I think back to that day and all the special experiences leading up to my eighth birthday, it's clear that I was given two life lessons . . . to put trust in the universe and to always put trust in my loving family . . . who, by the way, never forgot any of my birthdays.

104°

Iт was early in the morning, and my aunt had the radio on in the kitchen. "La India," a song about an Indian girl lost in the desert was softly filtering into my dream . . . I was riding a pinto horse bareback through a desert in full sun. The horse was sweaty and so was I. The blinding glare from the sun was bouncing off the white sand . . . and I was wondering if the song was part of a mirage or my dream. Then I heard my sister's voice . . .

"One hundred four degrees! We're going to melt."

Immediately, I woke up in a pool of sweat. I had thrown my pillow and all the covers off to the side of the bed. My hair was soaked, as if I'd just gotten out of the shower.

"*Amigos, la temperatura va llegar a 104 grados. Ya llegó La Canícula,*" the radio announcer was saying. (Friends, the temperature will reach 104º. The heatwave has arrived.) Well, that explained all the sweat.

I dripped out of bed, feeling a bit grumpy from being so hot and sweaty but mostly because I'd noticed that Nene had already gotten up without me. That wasn't fair. I didn't want to miss out on anything.

As I stumbled into the kitchen, my aunt said, "*Buenos días. ¿Como dormiste?*" (Good morning. How did you sleep?)

I told her about how hot I was and that I'd dreamed I was riding a horse in the middle of the desert and it felt like I was on fire. She told me my sister had dreamed about being in a hot kitchen cooking over a stove, and she woke up all sweaty too. Tía said it was because the temperature had already reached 89° and it was only 7:30 a.m. The local radio station had officially proclaimed the arrival of the yearly heatwave, La Canícula. It was supposed to reach 104° by noon or early afternoon. If that was the case, she doubted they would let us run around outside too much; maybe by evening if it cooled off.

She handed me a bath towel and fresh clothes and had me take a cold shower and come back for breakfast. My sister had already cooled off with her shower, and I headed out the kitchen door for mine.

My granny's house had an outdoor toilet and bathroom. It was in a separate building behind the house. The toilet was on the left side, with its own separate entry. The right side of the building housed the bathtub. The concrete tub was the size of a small schooner and about two and a half feet deep. There were faucets that let out the hot and cold water, but if you wanted to shower, you had to clamp on an attachment that had a shower nozzle at the end of a rubber hose. Nothing like the shower we had at home.

The bath and toilet rooms had another unusual feature—a three-inch gap at the top and bottom of the doors. I wasn't fond of using the toilet after dark. We never turned on any lights because Granny's bed was in a nook right next to the kitchen door and the toilet was just outside. Not wishing to wake her up, we'd leave the lights off and stumble around in the dark. Honestly, it wasn't the dark I was afraid of. I was afraid of the tarantula-sized spiders that scurried in after dark through those nice three-inch openings at the bottom of the doors. I usually opted to use one of the bedpans my granny kept under all the beds. In the middle of the night, you could often hear someone tinkling into a bedpan. It was weird using one but much better than feeling a big spider running up your leg.

Anyway, as I sat in the tub, I held the shower nozzle over my head and let it run with cold water long enough to feel the desert heat leave my body. I'd done that at least a full ten minutes when my aunt knocked on the door to see if I'd turned into a prune. She gave me the good news that breakfast was ready.

Say no more. I finished rinsing off the soapsuds from my hair and, after I got out, rinsed the tub for the next person, as my granny had taught us to do, and got dressed. It was so hot in the bathroom, even though I didn't have the hot water running, that I still worked up a sweat getting dressed.

When I walked in to the kitchen, I was greeted with a big smile from Tía Lolis. The table was set and ready for us to have a great breakfast. Because of the intense heat, Tía made a *licuado de sandia*, a watermelon ice drink, instead of coffee. It's a refreshing drink that is simple to make. It is just watermelon, water, and a bit of ice, mixed in a blender. You can make it with any kind of fresh or frozen fruit. Never one to refrain from cooking in a hot kitchen, Tía had made flour tortillas, scrambled eggs, and bacon, with the ever-present refried beans. Of course, Bueli added her homemade pickled jalapeños to the beans. Nothing ever kept her from eating hot peppers.

We must have been pretty hungry because there wasn't much talking going on. One of my favorite things was and still is homemade tortillas, either flour or corn. My aunt's flour tortillas were extraordinary. They were soft and chubby. And if you put butter on them, they melted in your mouth.

After the food was pretty much gone, we got up from the table. A little burp escaped from my sister, which was hilarious because she was a delicate eater and quite picky. On that morning, she ate like a truck driver.

We helped by clearing the table and washing the dishes. Bueli grew a special type of gourd that, when dried, was used as scrub pads and as wash cloths. They were called *estropajos* (loofas). We used them at home too, so Bueli always made sure to pack some in our suitcases before we went home.

The bulk of the day was spent on the front porch listening to the radio, keeping tabs on the weather report, and playing card games with my aunt. By three in the afternoon, the heat had crept down to 103°. We sat in rocking chairs fanning ourselves with oriental paper fans. Tía Lolis suddenly got up and went in the house. She came back out with an umbrella and a coin purse and told us she'd be right back.

Bueli came out and asked us where Tía had gone, but since we were clueless, we shrugged our shoulders. About ten minutes later my aunt turned up with a big grin on her face, went around the back of the house, and then emerged with a big metal tub. She had us move our chairs closer to the tub.

Moments later, a man came up to the gate and said, "*Hielo, hielo, Señora.*" There was a tiny man holding a block of ice more than half his size with metal prongs. My aunt waved at him to come in, pointed to the metal tub, and told him to put the ice in the tub.

Then she told Nene and me to sit back in our chairs, take off our sandals, and rest our feet on the block of ice. We let out a squeal because it was so cold but instantly felt the heat leaving our bodies.

TÍA LOLIS, THE GREAT ENTERTAINER, PLAYING HER GUITAR
TO TAKE OUR MINDS OFF THE TORTUROUS HEAT ON A SUMMER DAY.

Bueli came out to see what all the fuss was about. She shook her head. That was something she'd never seen before. "*Pues ya tenemos aire acondicionado*," she told my aunt. (Well, we now have air conditioning.) And she was right. Bueli placed two more chairs around the tub. She sat down in the chair next to me, took her shoes off, and joined the ice circle. When my aunt came back, she was carrying a tray with four pineapple sodas and four tall glasses with ice. Tía passed them around like a cocktail waitress saying, "*Señorita, Señorita, Señora.*" Then she sat in the chair next to my sister, took her shoes off, plopped her feet on the ice, and let out a big "AH."

As we sipped our ice-cold pineapple sodas, we felt the temperature begin to cool a bit. We could see on the thermometer that it was now down to 102º, then a little later 99º, then 95º. . . . And as the day went into early evening and our ice was melted, my aunt went in the house to make dinner.

We ate a light meal that night, fresh figs we had picked the day before that had been chilled in the refrigerator and cheese.

After our evening meal, Tía brought out her guitar and started to strum a few chords and crack a few jokes. She was quite an entertainer and pretty good with the guitar. After playing for an hour or so, she saw we were starting to nod off and decided it was time for us to get to bed.

It wasn't that late, but the heat of the day had taken a toll on our energy, and we were all a bit tired.

Tía told us that we were going to have a special treat. She and Bueli went to the backyard and disappeared into their storage shed. They came back out, hauling four army surplus cots.

They said it was too hot to sleep inside the house tonight, so we were all going to sleep outside in the patio. "*Vamos a pasar la noche en el campo debajo de las estrellitas,*" my aunt explained. (It will be like spending the night out in the country under the little stars.) But I felt like we were sleeping under the watchful gaze of the whole universe. This was something else I never did back home.

My aunt had us brush our teeth, get into the coolest pj's we had, and pick out our cots. Once she and my granny were ready for bed, they came over and tucked us in with a pillow under our heads and a lightweight sheet to keep the mosquitoes off.

In spite of the extreme heat that made even sitting in the shade a challenge, it seemed like our whole day had been a series of special and unexpected treats. I noticed, even though I was only seven years old, that my granny and aunt never stopped giving; it was their true nature. And I knew I had many things to be grateful for, which I acknowledged in my own way when we said our evening prayers together.

Finally, as the evening began to cool down and the noises of the day began to fade, we all drifted into a deep slumber under a starry sky.

Dripping Springs

Sure, it may have been the early seventies, a time for rock concerts, love-ins, peace marches, flower power, free love, Haight-Ashbury, long hair, counterculture, and anti-establishment, but for me, it wasn't quite that colorful.

My nose was always pretty much connected to the grindstone. Not that I didn't have a few interesting adventures . . . I did, trust me. But they didn't revolve around any of the big music scenes that were part of the late sixties and early seventies. I was never a regular at the Fillmore West or the Avalon Ballroom. Not even close. Though I'd never been to a concert at either of those places, I knew plenty of people who had. In fact, I hadn't been to many concerts at all.

I was a college student in Austin, Texas, at the time. Although I was connected to the counterculture, anti-establishment, hippie-love, and peace movement, I just never went to any rock concerts. They always involved paying to get in.

Knowing where Austin's famous honky-tonk bar, Threadgills, was located was my strongest connection to local music history. Did it count when you heard a concert blasting out of Armadillos while sitting outside in its beer garden listening to music, secondhand? I seriously doubt it.

But the time I went to Willie Nelson's First Annual Fourth of July Picnic in Dripping Springs, just outside of Austin, out in the hill country back in 1973 . . . well, maybe this story would count for something.

On the morning of Willie's Picnic, I got an early phone call from my longtime friend, Victor. I was barely awake and a bit foggy. As I forced my brain cells to kick in, I finally said, "Oh, it's you, Victor."

"Well, who else do you know crazy enough to call you at six thirty on a Saturday morning?" he questioned.

"Good point. Let me just get out of bed and wake up a bit. I'll call you right back." So I hung up, took the phone off the hook, and crawled back under the covers to take up where I'd left off. Victor was just going to have to call me later, much later.

At that time, I was taking summer school at the university so I could get ahead and graduate mid-term. I had just finished some exams and was totally exhausted. My three roommates, Heidi, Robyn, and Gracie, had all gone back to Brownsville to see their parents for a short vacation. I wasn't sure how long they'd be gone. As they drove off, they yelled out the window that they'd stay there as long as they could stand being back in the Valley.

By our second semester, we'd all gotten comfortable being on our own in a big college town. I suppose we felt like we'd outgrown our small hometown. Maybe we felt a little too sophisticated. The girls all told me they didn't want to shop in town on Elizabeth Street as they had before or to revisit our old community college. They had already decided that, within a week, they would be bored and back in Austin.

I never gave much thought to going back to the Valley. I was plowing my way through college, hoping to come out with a degree. That was the first step. I had no idea about what my subsequent steps would be. So I decided the best thing to do was finish my summer classes and in between, rest, relax, and recharge. We had a pool in our small apartment complex where I made tanning and swimming my summer priority.

On this particular morning, my friend had broken the first rule in my book of etiquette. Rule No. 1: In polite society, you NEVER call someone's home before 9:00 a.m. on a weekday or 10 a.m. on a Saturday or Sunday. It's just not done. Didn't Victor's mom teach him any manners? Then again, Victor was a bit rough around the edges, so I imagined that wolves had raised him.

Two hours later, I was still in bed. I was trying to break a record and sleep for twelve hours straight. My previous record had been ten hours, but I thought this might be my record-breaking morning until I heard . . .

BAM, BAM, BAM on my front door. Someone was yelling, "Patti, open up. Are you okay?" BAM, BAM, **BAM!** The pounding and yelling continued. "Open up!"

I tossed off my covers, dragged myself to the front door, and pulled the drapes to the side just enough to peek at the madman who was pounding my door into a pile of toothpicks. Why was I not surprised? It was Victor. Man, I was irritated.

Unbolt the door, take off the security chain, unlock the door, and move away, I told myself. Go into the kitchen and put on a pot of coffee. Do anything but don't look at Victor right away, or you might say something you'll regret. Just breathe deeply and look away.

So that's what I did. I moved away from the door and started messing around with the coffeepot in the kitchen.

Victor came bursting through the front door when he finally realized it was already unlocked.

But I didn't keep my big mouth shut as I thought I could. I turned around, got right up to his face, and said, "What the hell do you think you're doing here? Trying to break open my door? What possessed you to act like a maniac? What, huh? What? First you call me at an ungodly hour, then this." I continued to rant. "What is wrong with you? What?" I persisted.

Then I let out one long breath. "Sorry, Victor." I immediately apologized. I wasn't a mean-spirited person. I was pretty much a marshmallow-pushover kind of a person that most of the time was accused of being too nice to people. I think Victor had startled me out of a deep sleep with all the pounding and it registered in my mind to react in a panic mode. "Honestly, I'm sorry, Victor. You know I didn't mean that."

"Of course, I know you didn't mean it, and besides, you're right. That was totally stupid of me to act that way and make it all dramatic like that. I don't know why I did that. It's not like anything bad could have happened to you. I mean, you said you'd call me right back and you never did . . . and then I tried calling you back, but your phone was either busy or off the hook so you didn't know I was trying to call. I know I look really bad in all of this." He stood there shaking his head in disbelief.

"I just put on a pot of coffee. Want some?" I asked.

He nodded his head yes.

"Okay then, grab yourself a cup. Then why don't we start all over, and you can begin by explaining why you broke rule number one in social etiquette," I said.

He took a deep breath and then began to apologize in his own way. "I forgot you had these crazy rules about social etiquette. You know what kind of a person I am; I have no clue about social etiquette. I mean, I came up here and just about destroyed your front door. I think the manager was about to call the cops when you finally unlocked the door. He must have figured it was okay. You know me, clueless. I'm truly sorry."

"Well, Victor, your apology is accepted, I suppose. Do you even know what my other rules for social etiquette are?" I foolishly asked.

"You mean there's more than one? You got to be jo-joking," he stammered nervously.

"No, my dear, I'm not joking. But I think my list is a bit long for you, so let's just drop it for now. Coffee's ready," I announced.

I looked in my refrigerator, and all I had were half a dozen corn tortillas, three eggs, half an onion, one tomato, a few jalapeños, jam, butter, milk, and half a loaf of whole wheat bread.

"Breakfast?" I asked.

He quickly took me up on the offer.

"Great," I said. "I'll make us some *huevos a la Mexicana.* Sorry I don't have any beans to go with."

"Hey, that's no problem for me. I like it all. I'll just sit here at the kitchen table and stay out of your way. Is that okay?" he asked.

"God, do I love my beans . . . oh well, this will still be tasty, but it would have been better with beans," I mumbled to myself.

I cracked open all three eggs and scrambled them in a bowl with a little milk, salt, and pepper and put them aside. Half of the onion, I chopped into very small pieces, threw in a little bit of butter and oil into a pan, and fried the onions until they were clear. Then I tossed in six tortillas that had been cut into small pieces, browned them with the onions, and finally added one chopped jalapeño, one chopped-up tomato, and the egg mixture. I cooked the eggs until they were well done.

Cooking always seemed to calm me down. It felt good to be nourishing my body as I'd been taught to do since I was a little kid. And it always felt more rewarding when I could share my food with a friend.

And, yes, Victor truly was a close friend. I had known him even longer than any of my roommates. He'd been there for me through bad breakups, through rejections, through trying financial times . . . he was a good person, even though he'd acted crazy this morning and sometimes he'd act a bit like a gangster. He had always been a trusted friend. But I'd been there for him too, many, many times before. When he was afraid his girlfriend of four years wanted to break up with him, when he got jealous of her male friends spending time with her, when he got angry with himself for his jealousy and self-loathing kicked in, it was hard to watch. We had been friends since high school, and for me, that was a long time. I didn't have any other friends from high school that I stayed in touch with. We had all gone to different universities or gone off to do other things.

"All right then, chow down, sir," I said, handing Victor his breakfast. I poured myself a second cup of black coffee and sat down to savor every bite of my huevos a la Mexicana. After I had finished, I asked him again, "Now why were you calling me so early in the morning and why did you come up here in such a panic?"

"Oh yeah. You got me sidetracked, offering me coffee and a homemade breakfast," he laughed. "Well, I heard about this crazy concert that's going to happen out on some ranch, like a mini-Woodstock. It's called Willie Nelson's First Annual Fourth of July Picnic at Dripping Springs, you know, way out in the hill country. You'll regret it if you don't go. You'll be so bummed when I tell you how good it was and that you didn't get to see Willie Nelson play. That's why I called you at 6:30 a.m., so we could get an early start and get there with plenty of time, maybe stop and pick up some supplies," he said enthusiastically. "So what do you say, huh? Do you want to go with me?" he questioned.

"Well, I'm not sure. Are we going to have enough time to get there? Are we going to be prepared for whatever might come up? Will we still have time to buy some supplies?" I wanted to know. "And besides, I don't have any money," I added.

"Patti, that was a simple yes or no question. Do you want to go with me, yes or no? Pick one and don't worry about the rest," he demanded.

"Well, I'll go if you promise me that we're going to have a great time and that you're going to make sure everything goes smoothly. Are you going to take good care of me? You know how I am. I don't want to go out to the middle of nowhere and get stuck or lost. It's just for today, right? We'll be back by tonight?" There . . . I had just laid all my conditions out in the open for Victor to either accept or reject. And I sat, sipping my coffee, waiting for him to decide.

Within seconds, he said, "We're going to have the best time ever. You won't regret it. You know me. I'll take good care of you. I always do, don't I? Trust me, you won't get lost in the crowd. I promise. Okay?"

"Okay. Promise accepted. I'll be ready in a few minutes," I said.

It didn't take me that long to get ready. I was in and out of the shower in less than five minutes. With my long hair dripping wet, leaving little puddles of water wherever I stood, I quickly threw on an old pair of jean cut-offs and a tank top I'd made out of a red bandana. I grabbed the multi-colored gingham shoulder bag my mom had made me, the funky straw hat I used when I was out by the pool sunbathing, and my leather huarache sandals. I was ready to hear what Willie Nelson had in store for us.

Since our morning had gotten off to a rough start, we were running late. We decided to get out of town quickly as we headed to Dripping Springs. Victor figured there would be lots of vendors selling all kinds of food and drinks, so we'd be fine. He always had plenty of cash on him; money was never a problem. I didn't want to know where he got all his cash since he didn't seem to have a job. Hmm . . .

The hour drive felt twice as long to me, but we did eventually make it. To my horror, there were hundreds of cars parked everywhere on this dusty and rocky caliche back road. Everyone had to hike in to the concert area. Victor parked his car in the first available spot, which was still at least a mile trek to the entrance, and we started to walk. It was sunny and starting to get hot. I was glad I'd brought a hat and had worn cut-offs and a tank top.

The concert was out on a ranch in a vast and barren open field with only one small covered stage for the musicians. I'd never seen so many people in one place in my whole life. Years later, I read in an article that the crowd was estimated at fifty thousand fans.

True to his word, Victor never let go of my hand because it would have been easy to get separated and lost. Don't forget there were fifty thousand swarming fans; getting lost would have been easy to do. And there were no cell phones back then, no GPS, no pagers, no remote anything. This was out in a barren field, no pay phones within a five-mile radius from where we were . . . nothing. If you did get lost, you were on your own. The fact that I didn't have two pennies to rub together made me even more anxious. If I got separated from

Victor, I wouldn't even be able to make a phone call. So to ease my mind a bit, I leaned over to Victor and said, "Hey, buddy, can you spare a dime?"

"A dime? What do you need a dime for? Are you serious?" he remarked.

"Of course I'm serious. What if I get lost in the crowd and need to make a phone call . . . to get a ride home?" I pleaded.

"You are not leaving my sight. Trust me. Nothing is going to happen. You'll be fine, and we'll be home by midnight," he reassured me gently.

"Yeah right, famous last words," I muttered under my breath.

Victor gave me a quick side-glance but said nothing about my slur on his promise. Instead, he maneuvered us strategically through the maze of crazy, dancing, stoned, and drunk fans and landed us a spot about forty feet from the front of the stage. I couldn't believe it. What a spot, perfect. We sat down in a small patch of grass and got comfortable in a fleeting chunk of shade that was cast by the stage.

I turned to Victor and said, "Thanks for bringing me."

He gave me his usual charming smile. "I couldn't think of anyone else I'd rather bring."

The atmosphere felt electric. Fans were milling about, checking out the scene, drinking, relaxing, and of course, smoking pot. Following a few more sound checks, Willie Nelson appeared on stage, and we all went wild.

I sat mesmerized. Willie Nelson was then, and still is, one of my favorite singers and songwriters. His voice was velvety smooth—rich, full, and voluptuous somehow, no sharp or irritating edges. And he had such a knack for timing and phrasing. His singing was like poetry to me. I loved it.

Victor had been right. I would've been bummed to miss Willie's performance. Then other greats started to appear on stage, singers I'd heard only on the radio or on an album—the iconic Kris Kristofferson and Rita Coolidge, who were a couple back then, and . . .

Leon Russell. What an insane voice he had; I had just fallen in love with Leon's deep, gravelly voice. And his long riotous hair . . . I appreciated that he had a distinctive, wild look. He sang songs off his latest release at the time, *Carney*, with such heart that it touched some private soulful part of me. I was spellbound with his singing and hardly felt the blazing sun on my mostly bare back and legs . . . hardly.

The day flew by with one great performance after another. There were so many singers that I can't remember the names of all the performers. I think Jerry Jeff Walker was there, maybe even Michael Murphy, but don't quote me on that since I haven't seen it verified in any write-ups on the Picnic. But then again it was so freaking hot I could barely remember my own name. I began to have a heat meltdown. We had brought nothing to drink or eat. How naïve was that. We figured there would be food vendors.

I tried to ignore the stinging I felt on my back and legs and tuned in to the incredible crooning of Charlie Rich. First, I thought what a classy voice he had; then I thought I was going to die of heat stroke in the middle of a ranch among fifty thousand people.

Someone give me some cool air to breathe. I'm suffocating!

I was starting to feel the heat in the worst kind of way, the passing-out kind of way, the getting-irritable kind of way. There was a nice hippie couple sitting next to us. We had struck up a conversation early on. They were big Willie Nelson fans and had no intention of missing out on this event, no matter how hot it got. The full-figured woman was named Shirley. She had strawberry-blond hair tied in a top-knot and wore a long Indian-print sundress. Bob, her partner of seven years, was a musician who played acoustic guitar in lots of Austin clubs. With dark-brown hair halfway down his back and a reddish-brown goatee, he had a sincere smile and an incredibly deep, contagious laugh. When they noticed I was ready to pass out, they handed me a cold drink and a handful of ice to rub on my forehead.

To put the time period in perspective, back in 1973, no one had water bottles permanently attached to their hips as we do now. Bottled water was what you bought if you wanted to have steam from your iron. You never carried it around like an accessory as we do today. I'm never far from my bottled water. I carry it with me at all times, at least 1.5 liters if not more. I even make sure I have bottled water for my dogs whenever we leave the house. Always. But back in 1973, never.

Here we were in the devilish Texas sun in the middle of summer on a remote ranch with few trees that I could see. What were we thinking? Even though lots of fans started to feel the effect of the sun's rays, it didn't slow down the flow of beer going around or joints that people freely passed. I was impressed with all the sharing.

The pot helped take the edge off my heat-induced craziness, but I stayed clear of the beer. I just wanted to drink some ice-cold water, or even lukewarm water for that matter.

My skin began to throb and ache. I knew I'd passed the point of no return . . . I was officially fried. Victor's glowing olive skin was basically immune to the sun; he never burned.

As we walked around looking for a toilet, as futile a mission as looking for a shave-ice stand, we heard a few more greats—Tom T. Hall and Waylon Jennings. After a toilet ordeal, we wandered back to our spot, which Shirley and Bob had saved for us. We sat back down and took in the scene. We had a little extra space as the folks behind us had left, so Victor and I were able to stretch out our legs.

After a few more hours filled with musicians jamming, the crowd giving standing ovations, and the cheering, adoring fans calling for more, the evening began to cool down. Victor and I hung around until way after dark. The whole experience was too great to walk away from. Even though I felt so burned, like I needed to soak in a tub filled with ice or roll around in a vat of aloe vera, I still didn't want to leave. It was my mini-Woodstock moment, and I didn't want to miss a thing.

But by nine in the evening, Victor decided it was time for him to get my badly sunburned body home. I reluctantly agreed.

That was a challenge. There were absolutely no lights out there. As soon as you wandered away from the stage area, it was pitch black. We had only the stars above us and the dark void in front of us and, of course, no flashlight.

Having a flashlight would have meant we were prepared. You could tell who'd been in the Scouts because they were the ones walking out with coolers and flashlights, folding chairs and beach umbrellas. They were the ones smiling and laughing like they didn't have a care in the world. They were the ones going straight to their cars and driving home.

The rest of us were stumbling around in the dirt, not knowing which direction to go. We were getting mad at our significant others for not having better planned our outing. You could feel the tension in the air. The high was wearing off. The music was far away. The good feeling was beginning to morph into irritation.

After wandering around in circles for who knows how long, Victor looked me straight in the eyes and said, "I'm so sorry. I have no idea how I'm going to get us home. I don't have a clue where I parked the car. I thought I'd be able to find it, but nothing looks the same in the dark. I'm going to have to come back in the daytime to find my car and so are half the people here. I'm sorry I didn't take care of you like I promised. Look at you; you're a mess. You're all burned. And it's my fault."

I was exhausted. My whole body felt like it was going to self-combust at any second. And, yes, I felt disappointed because Victor had promised to get us home and he'd let me down. I was pretty mad at him by this point, but I was madder at myself. I had no business depending on Victor. By this time I had totally tuned out Victor. I could see his lips moving, but I didn't have a clue what he was saying, and I really didn't care anymore.

There was nothing I hated more than to feel like the helpless female stereotype. But there I was, feeling exactly like a helpless female and worse—on the verge of crying.

Something inside me snapped. I turned to face Victor and said, "You're on your own, buddy. I'm outta here."

I turned and walked away. He ran after me and said, "You're just going to leave me he-here? We're not going to find a ride out of here together? Are you joking?"

"No, Victor, for the second time today, I am absolutely NOT joking. I'm sorry you didn't keep your end of our agreement, but I'm more sorry that I made any kind of agreement with you in the first place. I should have looked after myself and not relied on you to do it. Don't get me wrong. I'm not mad just at you; I'm mad at myself too. Don't call me. I don't have anything good to say to you, understand? Good luck getting home tonight." And with that I turned away again and ran to catch a station wagon I saw pulling away.

I ran up to the car. It was packed with about six people. I asked if they could squeeze in one more . . . told them where I lived and asked if they'd be passing anywhere nearby. The car door opened, and I hopped in. As we started to drive away, I turned to look out the back window.

I could see Victor's silhouette against car headlights. He was standing there, frozen, exactly where I'd left him. I felt guilty leaving him, but I knew for certain he'd have no problem finding a ride home. Just then a car stopped next to him, he leaned in to say something, then the door opened, and he got in. Did I forget to mention that Victor was drop-dead gorgeous . . . an Adonis of sorts?

As we drove off and were about half a mile out, after looking around the car, I realized I had just hitched a ride with six guys, who appeared to be either drunk or stoned. I nervously wondered if in my haste I'd chosen my ride wisely and if I wouldn't end up on some front-page headline.

My body arrived at my apartment safely from the car ride . . . but not from the concert. For three weeks after the debacle, my whole body peeled from the severe sunburn I'd gotten that day. I looked like I had some kind of skin disorder or was a monster that was molting.

Victor called every day, several times a day; I never picked up the phone. When my roommates got back, they got tired of answering all his calls and taking all his messages, either saying he was sorry or pleading for me to call. I wasn't ready to let him off the hook. I wasn't ready to let myself off the hook either.

My roommates had returned just as I'd imagined they would—after being bored at home and restless to get back to the city. They began to make plans about the traveling they would do once they finished college, and none of them ever mentioned going back to the Valley.

After one of my morning classes, I decided it was time to take a dip in our swimming pool. I got out my black bikini and took a look at my body. I realized that it had finished peeling.

That's when it hit me. If my body was finally over the sunburn, if it was done with the peeling and suffering, if it was renewed with fresh skin and ready for a brand-new start, then shouldn't I be able to do the same thing with myself and with Victor? Wasn't it time to stop punishing us both and move on? Was I not resurrected in a way?

The person that came out of that burned cocoon was not the same person who had entered it. This version came out with much tougher skin. Ready to fight for her rights, demand to have her voice heard, and yet ready to accept hardships with humility and forgiveness for herself and others. The new version of me was ready to forgive Victor for acting like a knight in shining armor and to forgive myself for acting like a damsel in distress.

With my swimsuit on, I marched out the door, ran down the steps, and took a plunge into the deep end of the pool. As I came up for air, I looked up and saw Victor standing right there, gazing at me. I got out of the pool and went over to him. He looked so forlorn and repentant I didn't want to make him suffer any more than I already had.

We stood there silently for a moment, looking at each other, then we simply hugged, and it was over. I grabbed his hand, and before he knew what had happened, I'd pulled him in to the pool. It was so much fun.

Victor and I had many adventures together before we finished college. I never knew what happened to him after we graduated as we disappeared from each other's lives. I always wished him well, had fond memories of all his kindnesses and loving attentions, and hoped more than anything else, that he'd gotten to marry his true love.

My roommates returned to the Valley after graduation, and they never left. They got married soon after they returned and quickly started a family.

Funny thing was I never did settle in the Valley. I went back briefly after graduation and then left, never to return. I moved far away from Texas across the Pacific and to a life I never could have imagined.

Pink Elephants

SOMETIMES WE LET OUR MINDS DRIFT into memories from the past, thoughts of the present, or dreams of the future. I think most people do that on a daily basis. The ideal is supposedly living in the present moment, but that is the most difficult to maintain, at least for me.

In writing about my past, I've had to dig deep and explore the memories. In doing so, I find a common thread has tied my life together. I see clearly now that every day of my life had been painted with the vibrant colors of my cultural heritage. Whether or not I was aware of it, there was no escaping. The only option was to embrace it.

Easy to say, now that we're in the twenty-first century.

The essence of this story will ring true to anyone that has felt the ugly face of bigotry, or perhaps just plain meanness. I know I have been fortunate in that whatever the world threw my way was mild in comparison to what some have endured. But to young children, the simplest of reprimands can be very painful. Awkward moments filled with self-doubt or awareness of how different they are from their peers can be traumatic. Each child's psyche is unique. How he or she processes the world's insensitivity is just as unique.

How do you teach a child to be prepared for jeers, teasing, or in some cases, senseless bullying? How do you teach children to defend themselves when an onslaught of sarcasm comes from an adult? I'm not sure I have an answer.

The only thing I do have is my memory . . .

When I was in first grade, my school, Ebony Heights Elementary, was a block away from my house. It was an easy walk to school every day and to home for lunch if I wanted. I was thrilled to finally be leaving the nest, at least for a few hours each day. I was well on my way to growing up.

My first grade teacher, Mrs. Phillips, was an older woman, rather matronly looking with her white hair done up in a bun and a simple dress, usually a solid color, and lace-up orthopedic shoes. Friendliness wasn't her strength. I'm not quite sure what her strength was. Maybe crowd control.

I suppose formal would be an accurate description for my teacher. There was nothing about her that was fun or warm as I recall. But teachers were different back then. There wasn't much fluff available. It was learning the basics every day, and that was it. The first teacher I had that was young, beautiful, and nice to all the children was Miss Ramirez, and she didn't arrive until the third grade. She felt like one of my big sisters.

Though my first-grade teacher taught us the alphabet and the beginning of math, she wasn't creative in the least. We were rarely given any opportunities to color or to learn songs in class. Mostly, our teacher stressed learning the alphabet and how to print.

My mind worked a little differently than some of my classmates. I saw that early on. And at times I felt embarrassed and self-conscious, but there was no one in my classroom to tell me that different was actually a good thing, that imagination was a premium, and that one day I'd look back on my life and say, "Thank God I was born with a little bit of spunk and a unique spin on reality. I'm different from the rest of the pack, and different is GOOD."

On one of those first grade days, Mrs. Phillips handed us a sheet of paper with an elephant mimeograph. She told us this was a treat for our break since we had been working so hard on the alphabet. She wanted us to color it in and have lots of fun.

Hmm, I thought, fun sounded good to me. Of course, I began coloring my masterpiece with pink, one of my favorite colors at the time. I decided it was going to be a female elephant, so naturally it had to be pink. If I had chosen to color a male elephant, it might have been blue or yellow or green. But it would be a girl, so pink it was. Once I had colored the whole elephant pink, I highlighted some areas with a darker fuchsia or a burgundy. Then the toenails were painted red, and I added black eyelashes, colored the eyes brown, and made the lips fire-engine red.

We all took about a half-hour to do our coloring. My friend Brady was a freckled and chubby boy who usually wore striped T-shirts and baggy pants. He sat next to me all the time, and we were becoming good friends. He was always nice and polite, never a bully like some of the other boys. In fact, the other boys would laugh at him when he had trouble running fast or climbing the jungle gym. I chased the bullies when they picked on Brady, but when they started to pick on me, I'd run straight to the teacher on playground duty. It didn't seem to bother me when they called me a tattletale or a baby; I didn't care. I wasn't going to stand around and let someone pick on us.

As soon as Brady took one look at my drawing, he said, "Gosh, that is so pretty. I bet the teacher is going to like yours the best. Mine is ugly. It's plain grey. You'll probably get a star on your paper."

He was right, I thought; mine was really pretty and colorful and happy . . . she was going to love it. But to be polite as we'd been taught, I thought of something positive to say to him. "But, Brady, yours is so neat. You stayed in all the lines, and you on put lots of grey crayon so it's real shiny. I think it looks nice."

He just smiled and said thanks, but he didn't look very confident.

Here we were, carefree first graders, coloring a mimeographed elephant for break time. Why were we worrying about approval? Who cares how a first grader colors an elephant. Aren't the students supposed to be encouraged to retain their identity and find their own voice? There's no right way or wrong way to color a damn elephant when you're a first grader. Actually, I firmly believe you can color an elephant any color you want to even if you live to be one hundred years old. Who cares? Art is art, and you can do whatever you please.

Well, my teacher, whom I will now refer to as Attila the Hun, started going around the classroom, taking the drawings from each student and giving each a careful inspection and critique. To my surprise, most of the kids had colored the elephant just as Brady had.

Attila said, "Very good, class, you've all done really well with your coloring assignment. The elephants are very realistic, neat, and—" She stopped when she picked up my paper. Looking at it with revulsion and disgust, she then continued to me, "Oh no, this is all wrong. Elephants are not pink. They are supposed to be grey. Why didn't you color it grey? Do you even know what an elephant looks like? You'll just have to take another sheet home and do it all over again in grey and bring it back to me tomorrow. Oh my!" She continued to bellow, "Well, class, *most* of you did very well with the exception of one or two students, but they will turn in a new one tomorrow, and we can see how well they listened to the assignment."

Assignment? She had never told us to color the elephant grey. All she had said was to have fun and take a break and color. It was supposed to be a treat. I didn't see what kind of treat it was to color an elephant grey. The other little girl that got in trouble for not coloring her elephant correctly was Debbie, who was petite for a first grader and painfully shy. I really liked her because we had a lot in common. I was pretty shy too but not as much as Debbie. Next to her, I seemed loud and pushy.

Her elephant had been all grey, but because she was so gentle with everything she did, she had barely pushed on the crayon. So it was grey, but just barely grey. I heard the teacher tell her to quit being afraid of everything, even afraid to hold a crayon.

That was a mean thing to tell her. Debbie wasn't afraid; she was a gentle soul. I felt like crying. Attila had succeeded in squashing our self-esteem; she squashed it just like she squashed the poor cockroach running across her desk. Grabbing someone's elephant drawing, she quickly rolled it up and . . . whack! Squashed cockroach, squashed self-esteem.

Before class was over that day, Attila gave Debbie and me our papers back and an uncolored sheet and told us to show the paper she was returning to our parents, to let them see what kind of work we did. She'd expect a perfect elephant tomorrow.

Fine, I thought. I'll show my parents the wrong elephant drawing and tell them how you want me to make it right. As rudely as a first grader could muster, I grabbed my paper right out of her hand. Debbie took hers only when it was handed to her, all the while keeping her gaze on the floor.

When I got home that afternoon from school, I didn't tell my mom a thing. I waited until my dad got home. He wouldn't let anyone push his baby around. Hard to explain know how I knew this, but I did.

Patiently, I waited for him to come in and relax a bit. But before my mom had supper on the table, I told her to come into the living room because I wanted to show them both something I had colored at school. My mom was so excited, she wiped her hands on her homemade apron and turned down the flame on the pot of beans she was cooking. She came in with her long-lashed eyes wide open and the red lipstick she wore perfectly outlining her full lips.

"*Ándale mijita, enséñanos*," she said. (All right, my little daughter, show us.)

I pulled out the pink elephant from my Big Chief writing tablet and held it up for them.

Oh my goodness, you'd think it was the *Mona Lisa*. They thought it was so beautiful. My mom actually keyed in on the resemblance. She told me that she especially liked the long black eyelashes, brown eyes, red lipstick, and red toenails, and then she winked. My dad said he really liked that too and not to forget the beautiful Mexican hot pink that I'd colored the elephant. He said, "*Puedo ver que ese elefante es una mujer. Que buenos detallitos hija. A la mejore algún día serás pintora.*" (I can see that the elephant is a female. Excellent details, daughter. Maybe one of these days you'll end up being a painter.) I was really pleased. I'd never thought about being a painter when I was in first grade, but maybe the die had been cast.

What I did next was nothing short of subversive. I took out the uncolored elephant and told my parents about what had happened. I told them verbatim what the teacher had told me and what she had told my friend Debbie. They were shocked to think that a teacher of young children would be so insensitive and cruel. My dad was probably mostly angry that someone would stomp on a child's creativity. We'd always been encouraged to express ourselves in any manner we saw fit. None of their children fit any one mold. We had extremely different features and personalities. We weren't your typical cookie-cutter-type kids. My oldest sister was a throwback to our Moorish/Spanish lineage on my dad's side—olive complextion with raven hair. Have you ever seen anyone who actually had natural, raven-colored hair? Hers was the only truly raven black I'd ever seen, and in the sun, it looked a dark blue-black. Then there was my next sister who was very fair skinned. A towhead until about the age of five, she was a throwback to my grandmother's side of the family from Puebla, Mexico. My brother was more of a blend of both sides.

Nene also got more from my dad's side of the family and had definite similarities to people from the south of Spain. Then there was me, who also turned out to be a blended type, maybe leaning more to my mom's side, but definitely more global looking. People never knew exactly what I was. Whenever someone asked me about my ethnic background, I always let them guess. They would say I was Italian, French, Jewish, Brazilian, or Greek but never Mexican. I thought that was really funny.

That's how it was in my family; we were all unique, never compared to each other, or made to feel like we had to match anyone else.

So when this coloring assignment took a nasty turn, my parents were on my side. They said I had done nothing wrong and that the teacher was completely in the wrong. If she had given explicit instructions from the beginning to color the elephant like a real one out on the savannah, that would have been a different story. But since she had indicated that this was purely for fun and enjoyment, then she was wrong. End of story.

They had me go grab my box of crayons and color the elephant exactly like I did the first time around. I asked them if they were sure about it, and they said they were, absolutely.

They got one of my sisters to call Debbie's parents and explain to them what had happened. They were surprised to hear the story because Debbie hadn't mentioned it. Her father was an elementary school teacher in the same school, and I think Debbie didn't want it to be uncomfortable for her father. She was very sensitive about things like that. My sister explained what my parents were going to have me do, and they agreed to have Debbie color her second elephant exactly like the first.

My teacher had a first grade rebellion on her hands, and she didn't know it.

The following day, I came in to the classroom with all the other kids and sat down next to Brady. Right after the Pledge of Allegiance was done, the teacher, standing in front of her desk, asked Debbie and me to come up to the front of the class and bring our new drawings. We proudly walked up together holding hands and with a grin on our faces. Attila looked a bit puzzled.

When we handed our papers to her, she actually let out a gasp loud enough that the whole class heard, and she had to go around to the other side of her desk to sit down in her chair. She sat there, speechless.

Where was her caustic critiquing now?

She never said a word. Instead, she took our new drawings and the original ones and went up to the board and taped them up with the others from the rest of the class.

My mom and dad had signed, dated, and put our home telephone number down on both my original drawing and the new drawing.

Debbie's parents had done the same thing.

Attila turned every color of red that was in a box of crayons.

She never bothered either Debbie or me again. Nor did she ever pick on anyone else who wasn't her own size.

Pretty Packages

First crushes are monumental, and if you're lucky, they can be larger than life and stay with you throughout your whole life. They're what all other crushes are compared to, just like first loves.

I remember my first crush with tenderness and a sense of humor because I was so romantic and so silly. I remember it with compassion for myself because I knew so little about love. And I remember it with gratitude because I was given an opportunity to grow.

His name was Javier, and he was the most handsome boy I'd ever seen.

I was a junior in high school, and he was a senior. When our paths crossed on the first day of school, I felt like I'd swallowed a flock of monarch butterflies en route to their winter home in Mexico. They had landed in my stomach all at once.

The phrase "eye candy" hadn't been coined yet, but if it had, it would've been the perfect phrase to describe Javier. About five feet nine inches with light-brown hair and natural blond highlights, he had a Beatles haircut with thick bangs that came over his forehead and framed his light-blue eyes. He looked athletic but more like a tennis player than a football player. His fair skin, blue eyes, and long hair gave him the look of a Romantic poet. Put him in a white ruffled poet's shirt, and he'd look like Lord Byron. Javier had a mustache that was brownish-blond and well-trimmed. By 2:30 p.m. on our first day of school, he already had a five o'clock shadow. I know because I passed him in the hallway on the way to my English class. Together with his mustache and five o'clock shadow, he made the other seniors look like middle school boys.

I noticed that he dressed differently than the other boys, who were wearing jeans. He was in a white cotton, long-sleeved, button-down shirt, khaki-colored slacks, and burgundy leather Weejuns. It made him look more mature. Javier was older than most of the other seniors. He'd transferred in from a private school in Mexico to improve his English, as he'd be entering college in the United States the following year. The year before, he'd lost his parents in a car accident, so he moved to Brownsville to live with his grandmother.

That's how the first day of my junior year started, with a monumental first crush.

Influenced by the emotions of my infatuation, I found the instances in which I acted silly far outweighed the times I acted with any decorum. The early part of the semester was spent wondering if I'd get to see Javier between classes or at lunch or how I could meet him. I place blame for having wasted so much energy on a crush on being sixteen. I suppose that was what sixteen-year-olds did in 1968. We didn't have many avenues to resolve crushes. You had to be formally introduced somehow or be in a class together. It certainly wouldn't happen that way in today's world. Everything that was once private is now likely to be instantly posted on some sort of social networking website and broadcast over the internet.

On any given day, if I caught a glimpse of his pale-blue eyes and we made eye-to-eye contact, he'd give me a big smile, and I'd immediately look down at my books, glance across the hallway in the opposite direction, or dart into the girl's bathroom, completely ignoring his smile and being aloof. If I'd blushed from one of his smiles, then I would avoid that hallway for several days in a row. Silly things like that.

My best friend, Lydia, was there to help me through my junior year. We shared our private thoughts and fears without hesitation. As well as being my best friend and confidante, she was also my algebra tutor and chauffeur because she was the only one in my circle of close friends who had a car and a driver's license. If she wasn't spending the night with me on the weekend, I'd be spending the time at her house.

Lydia had a crush of sorts too on Bennie. Maybe her crush was not as bad, but it was a crush nonetheless. Bennie was a completely different sort of boy—short with a crew cut, wore horn-rimmed glasses, and was on the homely side. What he did have going for him was an attractively high IQ, bordering on genius. He excelled in math and science. He was a good match for Lydia because she was also brainy. Though she knew Bennie because they were in calculus together, they never talked as they were both very shy.

If Lydia and I had a light homework load for the weekend, we would pile into her big Ford station wagon on Saturday morning and go window-shopping downtown or to the beach at South Padre Island to work on our tans. Padre Island was relatively unknown at the time. It wasn't the spring break destination that it is now. There were a few large beach houses belonging to old money, and scattered along the oceanfront were modest beach shacks, a few hotels and restaurants, but nothing major at all.

It did have miles of white sandy beach to drive on, abundant sand dunes, and gentle surf. We'd drive on the beach until we'd find a nice secluded dune and set up for a day of sunbathing with baby oil in tow and plenty of iced tea. I'd usually get a bad burn on my first attempt at tanning, but then I'd brown up. Poor Lydia was fair skinned and never tanned, just burned. I gave her credit; she never stopped trying to get a tan.

Even though we saw each other every day at school and talked on the phone after school about our classes and homework, our latest crises were always more important. My current crisis, how to meet Javier, was a top priority for Lydia. She loved playing Cupid. That day on the dunes she came up with a plan. Bennie was good friends with Javier. He lived a few houses down the street from Javier's grandmother. By approaching Bennie herself and on my behalf, Lydia could take care of both of our problems. She'd get to know Bennie better and have a chance to talk to him more than she had so far in class.

We both thought it was a flawless plan.

In spite of all the Javier thoughts swirling around my head, I remained focused while in class. It was important to me to keep up a high grade point average. I had my sights set on going to our local junior college first and then transferring to a larger university. That would be the only way I could afford to go to college. I knew some of my wealthy friends would apply to a big university right away and go there as freshmen. I wanted to apply to the bigger universities all over the country for my own satisfaction, to see if I would be accepted, but I had no intention of going. At least not right away.

It made sense to me to stay home my freshman and sophomore years at our junior college, work really hard for straight A's, and transfer all those A's to a university. I had heard too many horror stories about kids who went away as a freshman to a big university and failed miserably. They weren't mature enough to handle the sudden freedom away from their parents.

Underneath all my crush madness there was focus, aspiration, and determination.

It was six weeks until the senior banquet. I still had not met Javier, though I continued to dream I would. Months had gone by in our junior year, and Lydia had still not implemented her plan. That's how crazy crushes were back then. She would freeze up in calculus and never speak directly to Bennie. She had no problem talking and joking around with any of the other students, but Bennie sent her into a tailspin. Lydia couldn't get up the courage to go to Bennie and just start talking. She had excuses—there wasn't an opportunity because the teacher started talking right away, or Bennie would be the first one out the door when the bell rang, or the teacher would ask Lydia to stay late after class to talk to one of the students who needed to be tutored. Her excuses were seemingly endless.

The bashful smiles between Javier and me continued in the hallway. That was torturous for me. Occasionally I could almost swear he came close to letting out a "Hi." But I was never sure, and I didn't want to be the first one to say it.

After months of angst and torment, I decided to take control of my destiny. One day after English, I knew I would be passing right next to Javier, who was headed in the opposite direction. This routine had been going on all year. I usually walked past him as he rounded the corner by the girls' bathroom. This time, I decided that at the exact moment I saw him round the corner, I would accidentally drop all my books. Guessing that he was a gentleman, I thought he'd stop immediately to help me pick them up. We'd both bend down at the same moment, look into each other's eyes, and then . . . well, the rest would be history, right?

So there I was, walking ever so slowly, trying to make sure I timed it right. I needed to be near the corner the moment he came around. As I downshifted my miniature-sized steps into first gear, with every slow-motion step I took, my books began to feel like they were made of lead. I felt my heart racing and pounding loudly and feared it would tear a hole right through the elegant white linen, double-breasted coatdress I wore.

When I caught a glimpse of Javier coming around the corner, I dropped all my books. Perfect timing . . .

Except that sandwiched in between Javier and Bennie were two pretty girls who were also seniors. Oh man, how could that have happened? Bennie quickly bent down to help me pick up my books and told Javier and the two bombshells to keep on going; he'd catch up with them later.

Bennie sweetly introduced himself. He didn't make too much eye contact with me, though. He said he knew my friend Lydia and that they were in calculus together. He wondered if I could help him out.

What? Me help him out? For what?

He quietly asked, "Do you think Lydia would like to go with me to the senior banquet? Could you ask Lydia, if I ask her, would she say yes? I bet someone already invited her. I mean she's so nice and smart and funny. . . . Well, I'll meet you here tomorrow. Can you see what she says? I'm sorry I'm asking like this, but it's like destiny. I didn't know how I was going to do it. As soon as I came around the corner and saw you'd dropped your books, man, that was cool. I mean, not that you dropped your books, of course, but that I could talk with you and have you as my go-between. You know, like the characters in all those books we read in advanced English class. Well, I'd better let you go. See you here tomorrow, same time. And thanks again for checking."

He barely gave me enough time to let out an answer. I yelled at him as he was running down the hallway, "Sure, see you tomorrow. And thanks for being such a gentleman, helping with all my books . . . ," I trailed off. He had already run down the hallway and was out of sight.

I think I was in a bit of shock. There I was, planning to take control of my own destiny, and just like that, destiny took control of me and showed me who was boss.

It got me wondering about destiny and if there really was such a thing. I thought about it as I walked to my next class and for the rest of the afternoon. Bennie seemed to think destiny had played a hand in the fiasco. He figured it was destiny stepping in to help him get a date. If it had been destiny, why hadn't it helped me out? My plan had backfired. Maybe it wasn't destiny. Maybe Bennie just saw an opportunity to act and acted upon it without hesitation. Maybe Bennie wasn't as shy as we all thought. I mean, that was pretty gutsy and smart too, to see my books all over the floor and to interpret that as an opportunity. No doubt about it, he was definitely smart. I was definitely not as smart; at least that's how I felt at that moment.

I'm sure I didn't hear a word the teachers said for my remaining classes, and I was still trying to figure out exactly how destiny worked.

Lydia was giving me a ride home that day since I'd forgotten to get money for the school bus. I waited until she'd dropped off two other friends at their houses and we were alone.

I gave her a rundown of what had happened after English. I could see she felt bad for me; Javier hadn't been alone, and he was walking with two of the most popular girls in the whole school. But her excitement over Bennie's proposal . . . well it was impossible to contain. She started to shriek in an annoying high-pitched voice that I'd never heard before. This didn't even seem like the Lydia I knew.

Then she began with the questions, "He didn't say that, did he? No way. He wants to take me? No way. Really? He said that? Tell me again what he said and start all over from the very beginning when Javier comes around the corner."

I thought she'd never stop hounding me. I had to keep reliving my failed attempt at controlling destiny. Worse yet, I had to keep seeing Javier come around the corner with those two Barbie dolls. And though I was considered by most of my peers to be quite a catch, I was no Barbie doll.

Lydia carefully thought out what she wanted me to tell Bennie the following morning. When she got home, she called me right away to quiz me on what I was going to tell him to make sure I didn't mess it up. My mom commented, *"Lydia apenas te trajo a la casa y ya te está hablando por teléfono. ¿No tienes tarea?"* (Lydia just dropped you off from school and she is already calling you on the phone. Don't you have any homework to do?)

Of course, it was obvious, but I told my mom we had some assignments to go over and I wouldn't be on the phone too long. Lydia kept me on the phone for an hour, having me tell her several times what Bennie had said, exactly how everything had happened, what I was going to say . . . she made me rehearse my lines until she was sure I was not going to ad lib and I'd answer exactly as I had been instructed. Her incessant coaching left me feeling exhausted.

The next morning Lydia picked me up for school so we could rehearse in the car. I repeated my lines once and then said, "Lydia, that's it. I'm not repeating your silly lines anymore. I won't mess it up, trust me. You're starting to give me a headache." And I didn't say another word all the way to school and kept looking out the window. As soon as we got there and parked the car in the student parking lot, I got out and walked ahead of her and made sure she didn't catch up to me.

There were some odd feelings beginning to surface, and I wasn't very proud of them. Even now I'm a bit ashamed to own up to them. But I think there was some envy going on. Somehow it didn't feel right that my plan had gone wrong and that Lydia, who had no plan at all, ended up benefiting from my failure. There, I admit it. My feelings were petty, shallow, and selfish. That was pretty bad. Though I didn't admit anything to Lydia about how I really felt, I made sure I did my best when I ran into Bennie later in the day. I wasn't going to fail my best friend, even if I felt like an ogre on the inside.

Just as we'd planned, I walked down the hallway, waiting to run into Bennie. Would he be with Javier? I wasn't sure how that would all work out. As I came up to our rendezvous, Javier appeared with those Barbie dolls again. Bennie was trailing a bit behind them. He signaled to Javier to keep on walking. The girls he was with were Delilah and Norma, and they were both cheerleaders, big surprise. They had blond hair, wore lots of makeup, and appeared to wear at least a size C-cup bra. I, on the other hand, sported a dainty pixie haircut, wore only a touch of mascara and clear lip-gloss on occasion, and wore a size B-cup bra. No comparison. If a hot guy like Javier had a choice between a bombshell and a little pixie, I guessed he would go for the hot babe. Who wouldn't?

As soon as Javier and the girls were far enough away, Bennie asked, "Well, what did Lydia say?"

I paused a bit as she asked me to do; she didn't want to seem desperate. Then I slowly started with, "Well, she hasn't made up her mind yet. She got a few invitations last week. She's pretty sure she is going to say no. Could she let you know tomorrow? Would that be okay?" I asked innocently.

"Well, I guess so. I mean is she even seriously considering my invitation? Because if she's not, well then, I guess I can ask someone else," he said sounding a bit hurt.

"Of course she is, Bennie. She just has to figure out a way to say no to some other friends without hurting any-one's feelings," I responded quickly.

The worst thing happened; I had to ad lib. Lydia told me precisely not to ad lib, and there I was, making the rest of it up. I wasn't very good at this. I've never been good at responding under pressure like that. I'm good if I've had time to think about an answer but never off-the-cuff. I don't do spontaneous well.

"Once she's done that, she'll be ready to say yes. I'm pretty sure of it. I mean, don't quote me on that or anything. But yeah, I think she'll go with you. If you want, I can ask her after our last class and maybe give you some kind of signal as you and your friend are getting on the bus. How's that sound?" I felt like I was groveling a bit here, but I didn't want to blow it for Lydia.

"You'd do that for me? Wow, thanks. That would be great. If you nod yes, then I'll ask her tomorrow before our calculus class. See you after school," he said as he walked off to catch up with Javier.

I had to wait until PE class to see Lydia again. I replayed everything that had happened. I think Lydia was genuinely surprised at how quickly her plan had gone out of control and failed to get her the results she had anticipated. Of course she told me to nod yes when I saw him on the school bus at the end of the day, and I did. And that was that.

When we got in the car, the only thing she said to me was, "You ad-libbed." She didn't say another word. Her introspective look spoke volumes. Nor did she call me that night. She had always called me before. I felt sick.

Sensing that Lydia wouldn't be in any mood to offer me a ride, I took the bus to school the next day. I knew she blamed me for things getting out of hand, but it wasn't my fault. Bennie didn't react to the rehearsed speech as she thought he would. I knew it wasn't anyone's fault, but that didn't make me feel any better.

There was nothing left to do. Lydia would just have to stew all day until her calculus class to see what would happen. I felt for Lydia, honestly. But I felt bad for myself too.

I walked to my next class in a bit of a daze, sick of all the games we were playing, and I just didn't care anymore. Having a crush on someone no longer felt as exciting as it had the day before. After being a participant in the Lydia and Bennie drama, it all seemed too complicated and silly. My heart wasn't in it anymore.

Then it happened. Javier came around the corner. He was walking alone, and he stopped dead in his tracks . . . right in front of me. I tried to walk around him because I was lost in my thoughts. He stepped in front of me again and introduced himself. He said he was sorry it had taken him so long to actually say hello and could he walk me to my next class?

I simply nodded yes like a zombie.

He walked right next to me as if we'd known each other our whole lives. Without any warning, that's exactly what it felt like, totally comfortable. As I looked into his soft blue eyes, I no longer felt overwhelmed with his good looks. I saw only this sincere person with a gentle way about him. He was so soft-spoken and polite.

He told me that Bennie was going to ask Lydia to the senior banquet and wondered if I'd consider being his date so we could double date. He said he wanted me to think about it because we didn't even know each other, although he felt like we did, and gave me a huge smile. It was the same genuine smile he'd given me on the first day of school.

I decided I wasn't going to play coy; forget the stupid games. So I blurted out, "I'd really enjoy getting to know you better, so yes, I'd love to go to the senior banquet with you."

"Wow, that's great. I'm so happy. Can I have your home phone number, and I'll call you after school?" he asked.

I wrote down my number in his notebook and then went into my English class as he bolted down the hallway to his next class. I was certain he'd be late for it.

I know exactly how it feels to float on a cloud, and it's exactly how I felt the rest of the day.

All went well for Lydia. Bennie invited her to the banquet, and she was back to being her effervescent self. Lydia was amazed how destiny had worked in my favor, too. I felt like destiny was highly overrated.

Lydia never said she was sorry for acting weird. I suppose she was embarrassed, and I understood that too.

The next couple of weeks were spent trying to figure out what to wear and all that girly stuff. My mom came to my rescue as she always did and helped me pick out a beautiful fabric I'd seen at the store the year before. When I first saw the material, it was way too expensive, and my mom had told me to not even look at it. It was simple enough, dotted Swiss, which I loved, and with designs of small bouquets of flowers in pastel shades of aqua and green. By the following year, what was left on the bolt had been drastically reduced, and there was enough yardage for my mom to make a simple floor-length dress. Bonanza. Or was that destiny poking around?

I used my favorite dress pattern. It had an empire waist with a ribbon under the bust that tied in the back, a low-scooped neckline with a ruffle around the neck, and small puffed sleeves. We chose an aqua-colored velvet ribbon for the tieback. I knew it looked a bit young and unsophisticated, but I didn't care. It was me. It made me feel like a princess. I had my own style and knew what worked for me. My mom had always tailored our clothes. She knew that, over the years, I had developed my own style and all she could do was try her best to help me achieve it, if we could afford it.

The last few weeks of school were some of the best weeks of that whole school year. Javier would walk me to class when he could, and he and Bennie would sit with us sometimes at lunch. But mostly, Javier would call me at night, and we'd talk for a while.

The night of the senior banquet finally arrived. We'd made plans to go out dancing after the event to the Drive Inn, a respectable nightclub across the border in Matamoros, Mexico. It was actually a very upscale restaurant and bar at the time. Many seniors were going there to continue the party.

Bennie and Javier picked Lydia up first. Since I lived closer to the high school where the banquet was being held, I was the last stop. I thought Bennie looked sharp in his black tux. Lydia wore a sleeveless lime-green floor-length gown with a silver beaded trim around the collar, and long white opera gloves. Her hair was up in a twist with two curls on either side of her face. Her outfit made her look a bit matronly, but it really didn't matter because Lydia was beaming and Bennie looked proud to be her date.

Javier looked sophisticated in a light-blue tux with velvet trim on the side of the pant leg. His shirt was a pastel aquamarine and had a ruffled bib and an aqua-colored cummerbund that coordinated with my gown. He looked like a tasty piece of pastel-colored Easter candy. His eyes actually seemed to light up when he saw me walk into the living room. My dress was perfectly tailored, and I knew I looked cute. It had a youthful, fresh look. My hair was still cut in a short pixie style, which suited my small features. I'd gone out on a limb by wearing a little makeup, a touch of brown eye shadow to highlight my brown eyes, a bit of black mascara to make my naturally long eyelashes look even longer, some pink blush, and cherry colored lip gloss. That was it. My mom gave me a light spray of her Chanel No. 5 perfume.

The senior banquet began in an uneventful way, actually. We sat at the table and talked a bit. Bennie and Lydia seemed comfortable with each other; of course, they'd spent all year in calculus together. Javier and I had spent only short spurts of time together and spoken on the phone after school. I began to sense this sick feeling in my stomach like things weren't going as well as my overactive imagination thought they would. I'd waited so long to meet Javier, to get to know him, to spend time with him, and even had wondered if I'd be his girlfriend one day. Something was missing, and I didn't know enough about life to know what it could possibly be.

When the banquet ended, I was relieved. I hoped that by the time we got to the Drive Inn things would start to heat up. We finally arrived at the restaurant and saw that most of our other friends were already there. Still hungry, we got straight to the business of ordering: *taquitos al carbón, carne asada*, and drinks. The taquitos were delicate. The tortilla had been fried to a crispy texture, not at all greasy, and the smoky meat dish was spicy and sizzling hot, everything my date was not.

We all got up to dance. Javier and I were quite debonair, a perfect match. If you were judging compatibility by how pretty we looked together, by how color coordinated we were, by how balanced our bodies were with each other, you would have sworn we were an item. Javier was totally sweet, polite, and an absolute gentleman. He was as close to being perfect as a person can get without genetic modification. But my stomach no longer felt queasy; there were no butterflies, nothing at all. What was going on? As we danced with all the other seniors, I tried to figure out why I felt nothing special.

Then it hit me with the force of a baseball bat across my gut. I realized that for me, Javier was this wonderful person who was in a pretty package, and that was all he was for me. I had been lured by beauty alone.

The most important element that was tragically missing from my first crush was a spark . . . chemistry. I had no reference point for comparison. How would I have known what spark or chemistry was before tonight? There was no feeling at all. And though I knew Javier was beginning to like me a great deal, I felt intuitively that it was more as a sister than anything else. He may not have known that yet, but he'd soon realize, as I had, that there would never be anything more between us than a precious friendship. That would be fine with me. I realized I had begun to look up to Javier like an older brother. In reality, we had little in common, and as a date, I found him quite boring. We weren't cut out for each other.

What a revolting development. I had fallen for the pretty package and never once considered that I might find its contents bland or flavorless. I was sure he'd feel the same way about me sooner or later.

The year I had spent obsessing and dreaming about Javier was a lesson the universe was trying to teach me, attempting to send an important message. It became a recurring theme in my adult life. Hard experience to have when you're only sixteen. And if you are a hard-headed woman, as I was later in life, you occasionally have to open up a few pretty packages if only to remind yourself that sometimes the packages with ordinary wrapping can be much more fun and fulfilling and contain greater substance.

Javier and I continued to be best friends, and our friendship deepened even more over the course of the next several years. He went to college in my senior year, and every day when he got home from class, he'd call me and we'd talk for hours about his day, my day, homework, college, our future, our dreams, and oh yes, his new girlfriend who eventually became his beautiful wife.

My first crush, Javier, was also my first real grown-up kind of best friend, and that was the real treasure I found inside that pretty package.

Tamales de Navidad

SOMETIMES THE THINGS THAT HAPPEN TO YOU as a kid stay with you your whole life . . . and we can only hope most are happy experiences that you have fun remembering. Like the time my dad took me fishing out on the jetty or my mom invited me to help her bake some pineapple empanadas or my aunt showed me how to hand paint Easter eggs. Memories like that turn the corners of my mouth up into a smile. And for me, some of these experiences became family traditions and, of course, my own traditions as well. I'm not a kid anymore, but I still remember sitting at the dining room table with my mom, sisters, granny, and aunt making Christmas tamales as if it were yesterday.

Although I was born in a small town in South Texas, my parents were both born in Mexico, and we had lots of relatives who still lived there. Being far away from our roots meant our family relied on our mom, dad, and in particular, grandmother to instill in us knowledge, understanding, and appreciation of our cultural heritage.

Though they shared their customs and traditions with us,

they always insisted that we respect and honor the country of our own birth . . . like the time my sister and I came home for lunch from school and we could hear the television set going with what sounded like a baseball game. It was the World Series, and that meant only one thing . . . that my dad had flown like a bat out of hell across the bridge from Matamoros where he worked just in time for lunch with the New York Yankees. My sister and I got there right about the time they were playing the national anthem. My dad had us stand up and put our right hand over our heart while they played the whole song. He reminded us that we were Americans and to be proud of being born in America and show respect whenever we heard the national anthem. He wasn't joking either; he was dead serious.

My friends thought it was pretty funny. Their parents never made them stand up for the national anthem. But because my dad argued a good case for it, I thought everyone stood up for it. They just figured my dad was real strict. Well, he was strict, but that wasn't what was going on. It was really about tradition.

I was lucky . . . I know. I grew up seeing the beauty and virtue of blending both of my cultures and coming up with my own family traditions. That's the way it was in my life; I had a taste of both worlds. And because of that, I came away with a deep connection to my roots and a strong sense of who I was and what I was all about.

From all those traditions, the times that stood out most in my memory with special flavors and aromas were the holiday celebrations.

Mexico is a country that embraces festivals, celebrations, national holidays, parades, and religious holidays. Often the celebrations will run for days. It's always a big party, no matter the occasion. So the gusto for celebrating runs deep in my culture, and it was bound to rub off on me too.

I know that holidays are a special time for most families when you slip out of daily routines, humdrum chores, and everything ordinary and are reminded of how much you love your family and depend on their love and support. It heightens your appreciation for all those you love. You forget about old hurts or rivalries, and you remember the good in your friends and family.

Of those holidays, Christmas was the most special.

Early on Christmas Eve, my granny and aunt would come to visit us from Nuevo Laredo. They would hop on a Greyhound bus and take a long ride to the Rio Grande Valley. It was one of those awful bus trips that took an eternity to arrive at its final destination. The bus stopped in every little town along the way to drop off or pick up people. Somewhere in the middle of the journey, the driver would take a half-hour break at either a small diner or the bus terminal. Most passengers ran to the bathrooms, and the hungry ones ran to the food.

My parents picked them up at the bus station one Christmas Eve. We were just as excited to have them come see us for Christmas as we were about Christmas in general. Honestly, we might've been even more excited.

This is what you might have seen as they walked through the door . . . Nene and me running and screeching, "Bueli! Tía! Yay!" and throwing ourselves right into their open arms. After they'd stumbled in with us hanging onto them like ill-fitting coats, their bags and luggage in tow, they'd get comfortable and change into some fresh clothes, take off their nylon stockings, put on their house slippers, and then promptly put on their aprons. No time was wasted on any chitchat. Nope, the chitchat came only once the actual cooking process was underway. They started to shout out orders like two little drill sergeants.

Then the cooking marathon began in earnest . . . at least that's how I remember it.

They had come to help make our Christmas tamales and our holiday complete.

"Have chilies will travel" should have been Bueli's calling card. From home, she brought with her *rajas de chile rojo y chile ancho* (red chili slices and dried poblano chili). She started by washing the chilies and putting them in a pot with water to soak. When the chilies were soft, she'd remove the stems and half of the seeds. It was important to leave some of the seeds in for flavoring. Next, she'd put them on the stove to boil in a pot with water, salt, black pepper, and garlic. After they had cooked to the point of falling apart, she'd put them in a *molcajete* (a stone mortar and pestle) and mash them to a thick consistency. She'd then heat oil in a pan with a little more garlic to infuse the oil, toss in the cooked chili, and fry it until it turned a rich reddish-brown. The chilies were key ingredients for seasoning the pork and the masa harina for the tamales.

My mom had already cooked pork and the beans the day before. Tía Lolis started mashing the beans and cooking them down to a thicker consistency. And there were tons of beans too, so mashing was a big job. You could see what strong forearms my aunt had as her muscles started to get pumped up with all the mashing. This was pre-food processor days, so you had to mash beans with a special bean masher, similar to a potato masher.

Believe me, this was all planned out ahead of time. It was like watching an intricate ballet as they danced through the kitchen, each one knowing exactly what her part was and never once missing a beat. They were good.

And as soon as the beans and chilies began cooking . . . oh man, the aroma made me salivate. When you cook that many dried chilies, you get the pungent pepper fumes that make you cough and gag a bit, especially if you aren't used to hot foods. I loved everything about it, even the hot-pepper fumes. It just made me want to eat tamales even more.

A favorite thing for me was when we mixed up masa harina for the dough. My mom always pulled out her big black enamel baking pan that had handles on each side. It was at least six inches deep, the kind of pan you might use to cook a pot roast or a turkey. The neat thing was the pan was so large you could easily mix up the masa with the chili. We always had a turn at sticking our hands in the masa and mixing it for a while. The chili gave the masa not only flavor but also a nice warm color. Other ingredients were salt, hot water, and melted lard. I guess many people used lard back then. Big hunks of it got melted in a pot and then added a little at a time to the dough to make sure the consistency of the masa was just so, not too slippery, not too dry.

There was a constant mixing, sampling, and adjusting of flavors. The incredibly spicy aroma of the chili began to fill the whole house. The smell of those chilies cooking on our stove was unique and unforgettable. My granny always used dried red chile ancho that she had brought from Nuevo Laredo. She was a lady who was totally picky about her peppers. If she were still living, she'd be called a connoisseur of chili peppers.

The day before my mom had also cleaned all the corn-husks used to wrap the dough. That is also labor intensive; you have to separate them all and wash out the corn silk and any worms you might find. You wash and rinse several times. She would leave them in the refrigerator wrapped in cotton dishtowels for use the following day. When the chiles were close to cooked, Mami would bring out all the husks. She'd fill both sides of our double kitchen sink with hot water and put the husks in to soak and get soft and pliable.

The skill it took to season the pulled pork with chili peppers meant it was my granny's job. She had no exact recipe; it was all by taste and feel, the chili being a key ingredient. We just watched and apprenticed. Once everything had been prepped, an assembly line was set up on our large dining room table that had a Formica top. Now, you'd say it was very retro. It was perfect for the mess we would make.

As soon as we were coordinated enough to hold a cornhusk and successfully spread masa on the husk with a spoon, we were given a spot to work on the assembly line with all the grown-ups. It was a privilege to be allowed to work on the tamales. And it wasn't even about how old you were; it was about skill level. My oldest sister was never any good at making tamales so she never made it to the assembly table, though she most likely did that on purpose so she could just goof off. She wasn't big on developing or honing domestic skills.

But it didn't matter that she wasn't there to help; we always had plenty of willing hands. A few of us spread out the dough, a few put in the filling, and a few rolled up the tamales and secured them with individual ties. This went on for hours. Since there were five kids and four adults, we had to make a lot of tamales, especially because we were allowed to eat as many tamales as we wanted. There was absolutely no rationing.

Now, when I make tamales for my family during Christmas, I make enough for us to eat for days, even if you want them three times a day, and I usually do. I make more than enough tamales so I can share them with my friends.

Bueli made three kinds of tamales—pork, beans, and a sweetened version with raisins. I was never a fan of sweet tamales, but my mom absolutely loved them, so we definitely had them on the menu.

I'm a vegetarian now, so my tamales are made with butter, not lard, and no meat. Usually I will make three types:

beans, white cheese with green chiles, and a spiced vegetarian meat substitute. I've had some people say, "Hey, aren't you vegetarian? Why did you make meat tamales?" That's always funny. I fool the meat eaters. And I think it's due, in part, to my granny's recipe for flavoring the tamales with chile ancho.

Anyway, as we were spreading, filling, rolling, and tying up tamales, Bueli would load them up in the big tamale pot that held at least four dozen and start cooking. Each pot took about one and a half hours, so the cooking went on through midnight.

Before midnight rolled around, we observed another essential tradition, midnight mass at Our Lady of Guadalupe Church. Mami called it Misa de Gallo (Rooster Mass). For us kids, it was a struggle to stay awake. Though we usually fell asleep, it never kept us from going and trying to stay awake all the way through.

Midnight mass is filled with memories of thick clouds of burning incense, nativity scenes, beautiful organ and choral performances, and the mass in Latin.

On the home front, Bueli and Tía stayed behind . . . cooking, cooking, and cooking some more.

By the time we got home from mass, several batches of tamales had been cooked and cooled. Eating tamales and drinking a cup of hot *champurrado* on Christmas Eve after midnight mass was a tradition.

While we'd been at mass, Tía had made us *champurrado*. This is a traditional drink made any time of year, but it is particularly special at Christmas. It is a creamy, steaming-hot, thick drink made with masa harina, the same corn meal used to make the tamale dough (and corn tortillas). It has a consistency similar to porridge and is thicker than hot chocolate. My aunt made our champurrado by mixing the dry masa harina in a pot with milk, water, cinnamon, vanilla, and crushed *piloncillo* (unrefined whole cane sugar). After that was boiled to a thick consistency, she'd drop in several blocks of Mexican chocolate and stir it on a very low heat until the chocolate melted into the mixture. She would then use our *molinillo* (carved wooden whisk), rolling the stick between her palms. Twirling the whisk with its carved indentations on the bottom made the chocolate very frothy.

No matter how sleepy we'd been in church, the tamales and hot champurrado gave us a second wind, and we knew we'd get to open one Christmas present before going to bed. Naturally it wasn't a present from Santa because he hadn't arrived yet, right? Then we all went to bed.

Well, not quite all. Mami, Bueli, and Tía kept cooking the tamales. They stayed up as long as it took, which was usually most of the night.

The aroma from the tamales cooking in the kitchen drifted all the way back to our bedrooms; we enjoyed the smell until we finally drifted off to sleep.

As most children in the world do on Christmas Day, the following morning, we woke up early. And of course opening presents was always our top priority.

While we did that, Bueli was back in the kitchen making a batch of her special *tepache*, a beverage made from fermented pineapples. Mami had cut the pineapple beforehand and had it soaking in water and piloncillo for four days. So Bueli added the right amount of cinnamon and cloves and put it in our Frigidaire to chill. By the fourth day, it was slightly alcoholic. We all got to taste this popular drink for the holidays. I was never a big fan of tepache, but everyone else was. And since it was traditional, we brewed it.

The last thing my granny made for the holidays were the *buñuelos* (fried dough topped with cinnamon sugar) for dessert. These buñuelos were different from hand-rolled ones. She made them very light and airy. Her mix was a thick batter. She would dip a buñuelo mold into the batter and, like a donut, place it in hot oil to fry. After it turned golden brown, she dusted it in cinnamon and sugar. They were delicate yet crispy all at the same time and melted in your mouth as you ate them.

The only way my granny could get all the buñuelos made was to have us stay out of the kitchen. This wasn't hard to do because there were the five kids and our parents who had to open presents, so we pretty much forgot about all the cooking going on in the other room.

Once we'd finished opening our presents that were laid out under our five-foot Christmas tree that my older sister, Ana, had decorated, we drifted back into our small kitchen and hounded Bueli for a taste of freshly made buñuelos. She scolded us, saying, "*Sálganse de la cocina, nunca voy a poder acabar los buñuelos si me siguen molestando.*" (Get out of the kitchen. I'm never going to be able to finish making the buñuelos if you keep bothering me.) And she meant it . . . we were ordered out.

It all worked out, though.

Nene and I took our presents to the bedroom and admired the piles of presents like they were mounds of gold.

My oldest sister, Chachi, immediately got on the phone to her boyfriend.

My other sister, Ana, who always loved to help out in any way she could, put all her presents away in her room and went to offer to help get Christmas dinner on the table.

Papi opened his bottle of Chivas Regal and poured himself a holiday drink.

Mami helped finish the food preparations.

Nene and I stayed in our rooms, playing with our Barbie

dolls. My mom had designed and sewn whole wardrobes for the dolls with the leftover material she had from making our clothes. My favorite was a sleeveless A-line cocktail dress made with navy-blue wool and a light-blue satin lining. It looked like a Chanel design.

While Ana placed the dishes and silverware on the table, Mami brought out all the food, which gave Tía and Bueli a few minutes to freshen up and change clothes. Bueli put on a little rouge, her orangey-colored lipstick, and a splash of violet-scented cologne. Tía put on a mint-green dress with a floral print, some bright-red lipstick, and a quick splash of Bueli's cologne. They were both ready for dinner.

On the way back to the dining room, Bueli rounded us up from our bedrooms.

We gathered snuggly around the table. Papi asked my granny to please say a blessing for Christmas dinner. As she said grace, she looked around the dinner table, making eye contact with each one of us. You could tell from her watery eyes that her heart felt full. A few tears escaped from her tired eyes and moistened her cheeks.

As the platter of tamales began to circulate around the table, along with a plate of steaming Mexican rice, a pot of beans, a bowl of chili peppers, green salad, sliced bananas for the rice, and the ice-cold tepache, I joined in all the exuberant conversations that also began to circulate around the table. "How delicious the tamales are." . . . "Which is your favorite kind?" . . . "Can I have more bean tamales?" . . . "We need more sliced bananas." . . . "How about more chili peppers?" . . . "Would anyone like some flour tortillas?" . . . "Save room for buñuelos."

We'd only just begun our Christmas meal, and I was already feeling full—with emotion. Tears were just under the surface. As they quietly started to trickle down my face, I realized that I had been given something far more meaning-ful than toys. I'd been gifted with my family's heritage and traditions to keep close to my heart forever. My Christmas past would always be part of my Christmas present.

I still celebrate the Christmas holiday much as I did as a child, with my family and friends sharing a meal made with love and joy. Opening one present on Christmas Eve . . .

And eating the tamales I've made, just as Bueli, Tía, and Mami taught me to make. Family traditions, which can be the best things in life, should never end; they should be shared . . . with everyone you love.

The Cave

LA GITANA (THE GYPSY) WAS A wildly popular *tele-novela* (soap opera) in Mexico City one summer when my mom, Nene, and I were visiting my dad. The story line of the soap opera was about a woman who had been adopted by a wealthy landed family. Her father had sent her birth mother back to Spain in hopes of keeping her Romani/Gypsy blood-line hidden. And of course, like any good soap opera, the story got complicated when the daughter found out the truth and her life began to unravel.

Sometimes the story line in our own life can get a little blurry just like soap operas, where the story line of fantasy, dreams, or even someone else's life can cross over into our own, and our own lives begin to unravel as well.

As much as I didn't want to compare reality to soap operas, there were times when being a teenager felt a bit like living in one. So the lesson for me was all about asserting myself in my own life, just as the Romani woman had to learn.

Nene and I shared the addiction to this particular soap opera with our Mexico City girlfriend, Carolina. We all loved it and had fun talking about the latest developments in the woman's tumultuous life. We had great affection for the Romani culture. At the time, in Mexico City, the Romani were called Gypsies. That was the only word I had ever heard to describe Romani people. In fact, La Cuevita in Mexico City was the only place I ever encountered anyone of Romani heritage. I was intrigued.

As if lured by the fascination of this lifestyle, Carolina and her brother, Ruben, had heard about a bohemian club called La Cuevita (The Cave) that they said we had to go see. All their hip young friends were talking about it and flocking there on weekends. The attractions, other than authentic Spanish Flamenco music, were authentic Romani fortunetellers that came in only on Friday and Saturday. All her friends were swearing to the accuracy of the predictions they received.

We had discussed details the day before when we'd met at Sanborns for lunch. We had to go, Carolina had insisted, and we agreed. How could we miss the opportunity to have our fortunes read by a bona fide Romani fortuneteller? When we left Carolina and Ruben, Nene and I had great ideas on how to pull off the rendezvous.

The club was located in one of the poorest and most treacherous parts of Mexico City. The neighborhood was famous for the known criminals it harbored and its high crime rate. It was unsafe to enter the area at any time of day, let alone at night. Even local police officers avoided the area whenever possible.

The fact is that most of the kids flocking to La Cuevita, like Carolina and Ruben, came from relatively wealthy families. I found it hard to understand why so many kids would be risking their lives for Spanish Flamenco music, drinks, and fortunetelling. I figured they were either insane

or naïve. Carolina and her brother fell into the insane category, and I realized that my sister and I fell into another
category altogether. We were like sheep, blindly following
the herd into the unknown. At any rate, we all agreed we'd
go on Friday afternoon.

This is one of the few times we didn't tell our parents
what our plans really were. We told them the usual, that we
were meeting Carolina and her brother in La Alameda and
then we'd be having lunch at Sanborns and maybe go to a
museum or catch whatever production was currently being
performed at Bellas Artes, we weren't sure. I didn't feel good
about the deception, but we knew our parents would never
have given us permission to go. Because the city was still
relatively safe and trouble free, my parents generally didn't
worry about our outings.

The city's altitude played an important part in what I
decided to wear that day. Mexico City has a 7,300-foot elevation and is very cool, even in the summer. It felt good to be
in a cooler climate, a big relief from the South Texas summer
heat and humidity. I figured it might be pretty chilly if we
ran late, so I decided to wear my white Levi's and turquoise
acrylic sweater that had a black belt at hip level and black
trim around the neck. It had dramatic contrast and looked
sophisticated, I thought. Nene, who usually dressed in a
more conservative style, wore her Mod-style dress that was
chocolate brown with alternating turquoise panels.

After we'd gotten dressed, my sister commented on my
choice of pants, thinking white was ludicrous for going to a
"cave" bar, but I rolled my eyes and said the name was probably only figurative. Besides, I told her, if it got chilly by late
afternoon, I'd be nice and warm and her legs would be icy cold.

My mom gave us her ritual blessing as we headed out the
door. As we walked down the hallway towards the elevator,

we told her in a very casual tone that we might be later than usual if we decided to take in a movie, so not to worry. It doesn't feel good to remember the glaring omission.

And we had no idea what we were in for.

We met Carolina and Ruben in town and went for a quick lunch at our favorite place in the whole city, Sanborns, of course.

I remember lunch went by quickly as we wanted to get an early start. We all ate simple, quick food. Either that had to be the best cheeseburger and chocolate milkshake I'd ever had, or I was extremely excited about our excursion to La Cuevita and anything would have been just as memorable.

Following lunch, we walked down to the Zócalo, which is a massive cobblestone plaza of great historical importance in the center of downtown. It is there, at this exact location, that the Aztecs built their city. After the Spaniards invaded Mexico, they erected structures right on top of the Aztec pyramids, temples, and ruins as conquerors often do in an attempt to quench their insatiable lust to destroy the indigenous culture.

The Zócalo is surrounded by a massive cathedral built by the Spaniards, a multitude of ornate government buildings housing murals by famous Mexican painters, and many gold and silver shops selling jewelry and high-end crafts. We went to that area to wait for a bus to take us to the outskirts of the city.

After waiting a half-hour for a bus to appear, we all got on and were lucky enough to find two seats together so the four of us wouldn't get separated. The bus was a much older looking model than some of the other buses we'd been on before and gave a very bumpy ride. But that was quickly forgotten as our journey began.

During our ride, the neighborhoods became increasingly impoverished. It was not uncommon to see houses with only tin for the outside walls or with rusted tin for roofs. The streets became narrower and congested, and the bus began to crawl along slowly. The area appeared to be densely populated. All the while it seemed that we were climbing in elevation. I guessed we were going into the hills.

The houses were dilapidated, and the storefronts were dirty and in need of paint. There were stray dogs roaming the neighborhoods, children wandering the streets, and old people hobbling along with their canes. Except for the occasional outdoor marketplace with its bright colors from sunflowers, gladiolas, calla lilies, roses, gardenias, and other flowers, it was a dismal area.

After what felt like an eternity to me, we finally were nearing an area with more modern businesses and courtyards, and the streets began to widen a bit and increase in traffic. There was absolutely no respect for traffic laws; cars, trucks, motorcycles, taxis, and buses were speeding and weaving in and out of traffic as if it were a mad dance.

We hadn't realized how long we'd been on the bus until an old woman sitting near us in the back of the bus yelled at the driver that she wanted to get down. As she stood up, she straightened her hot-pink floral apron and grabbed a mustard-colored plastic grocery bag that was overflowing with fresh produce. She maneuvered her way through the crowded bus to the exit, and as she passed us, we heard her mumble, "*Ya son las tres y media, Dios Mío, se me hiso tarde.*" (It's already three thirty. Oh my God, I'm running late.) We realized we'd been on the bus for an hour.

The bus had to keep stopping to pick up passengers, and every so often it had to stop to let people off so it could take hours to reach your final destination. When you wanted to get off, you had to pull a cord that hung over the doors and made a loud buzzing sound, notifying the driver a passenger wanted off. But you still had to yell out "*Bajan*" (getting off). Then you'd be sure to be given ten seconds to get off. You really had to be ready to jump off the bus because it rarely came to a full stop.

My mind started to play games with me. I was getting worried that it was already 3:30 p.m. and we hadn't even found the club. I had no idea how late we'd get home. We'd never gotten home after dark, and if we were stuck taking a bus back home, we'd really be late. The glamour and excitement I had felt in the morning was starting to be overshadowed by fear. What were we getting ourselves into?

It wasn't hard to see why this place was considered so dangerous. You could feel some sort of threatening energy lurking in the bus, on the streets, and probably in the club too. I was beginning to regret coming with Carolina and Ruben, especially since no one knew where we were going. Maybe we were all insane.

Just as my paranoia was beginning to give me a headache, the bus stopped at a big intersection, and Ruben told us we had to get off. As I scooted across the seat to get out, I realized how dirty the seats really were because my white Levi's were no longer white. They were more like white with dirty brown and sooty black streaks across the back of my legs and my butt. My sister took one look at my pants, shook her head, and said smugly, "Like I said, ridiculous." And of course she'd been right.

We waited for the green light in order to cross the busy intersection, but somehow it didn't seem to make it any safer to cross—we still had to run for our lives. The zooming cars whizzed by, missing us by a few inches. I think I had turned sheet white by the time we reached the other side of the street, and my mouth felt dry, like I'd run out of spit due to the mounting tension.

Above a doorway, we saw a sign that read La Cuevita. At the entrance was a heavy arched wooden door. Once you were in, you walked down a winding staircase into an area that felt like a basement. It was very dark and damp and smelled both musty and smoky. I held onto the wall as I was going down the stairs and realized that it was actually a rough rock wall. It was a real cave.

We finally got to the bottom of the stairs, and there it was, a cave about twenty feet high, maybe thirty or forty feet wide, and I wasn't sure how deep because it was so dark and hard to see. On a stage all the way in the back, a man sat on a barstool playing a Flamenco guitar. He wore a black hat with a flat top and a large brim, a white ruffled shirt, a red silk sash around his waist, and tight black pants. The available floor space appeared to have as many bistro tables and chairs as it could handle, with three to four chairs per table; we were really crowded. There was a bar somewhere. My eyes had not adjusted to the pitch-black of the cave, and I couldn't see where it was, but I could hear glasses and cups being jostled about.

Thick cigarette smoke, along with the lack of adequate lighting, made it nearly impossible to see where you were going. I spotted only one or two wall sconces that looked medieval at best. I half expected to see a spiked ball and chain on a stick and maybe a few clubs and battle-axes mounted on the wall.

After fumbling around in the dark, we found a table and sat down. We ordered coffee and took a number so we could talk to the fortunetellers. Even though we'd gotten there in the late afternoon, the place was already packed with young people, all trying to look very sophisticated. I'm guessing most of them were as nervous as I was.

We sat in awe as we listened to the Flamenco guitarist. He played as though the music had its own life. It seemed to me the guitarist was the one being played by the music, rather than the other way around. The music was both passionate and lyrical and took us all on a roller coaster ride of emotions. And just when it felt as if the energy in the room had reached a fevered pitch, had reached a crescendo, an electrifying Flamenco dancer joined him on stage. Her beauty was partner to his musical storytelling. He played for her and she danced for him, and it was like watching a seduction told in dance steps and guitar tempos . . . her bold movements, lifting her yellow-and-black polka-dot skirt in twirling motions, her clapping castanets, feet stomping in rhythm to the music. Whatever we were witnessing was clearly seductive. The whole audience was sucked into the dance as if the smoke, the guitar, the beautiful dancer, and the dark, dark atmosphere had cast a mysterious spell.

Even if I'd never gotten my fortune read, that experience had been enough for me; the trip out to the end of the civilized world had been worth the Flamenco dance.

We had quite a wait before we saw the fortunetellers; many people were ahead, and it was obvious no one was in a hurry.

The waitress came up to ask us how we wanted our fortune told—with Tarot cards, crystal ball, palm, or Turkish tea reading. Ruben and I opted for a reading with Turkish tea, Nene went with Tarot cards, and Carolina chose palm reading.

Our waitress finally tapped my sister and me on the shoulder and pointed where we were to sit down. As I approached the fortuneteller, I was apprehensive; I didn't know what to expect. Maybe the she would look like the witch in *Snow White and the Seven Dwarfs*, the one with the big wart on the end of her large bulbous nose.

But that's not what I found. This woman had an elegant nobility about her. She wore a red-and-black paisley scarf over her long, flowing, jet-black hair. Her eyes were the color of exotic emeralds. She had a rather fair complexion and wore a black embroidered peasant blouse with a full red-flowered skirt. She gave me a big smile, nodded, and told me to have a seat. I couldn't help but notice all the gold she was wearing. She had huge gold filigree hoop earrings that came down to her shoulders, multiple thick gold chains around her neck, and gold rings with colored stones on all fingers of both hands. I didn't want to stare, but I couldn't help myself. I'd read fascinating stories about the Romani and their gold and thought it was a myth, but now I was sure there must be some connection to their gold and their magnetic power.

She handed me a white porcelain cup about the size of an espresso cup filled with tea and motioned that I should drink half of it and give her the cup back. Well, I did that, but not without effort as the tea was extremely strong and it tasted more like thick, soupy ground tea, not at all like regular tea. I handed her the cup. She took one look at the inside, made some sort of comment I didn't understand, then flipped the cup over into a deep saucer, closed her eyes, and sat silently with both hands on top of my cup. She waited for the tea leaves to drip down the inside of the cup. The seconds dripped by slowly, just like the tea leaves.

Once the cup had drained sufficiently, she turned it over and began to stare inside the cup, turning it in many directions and looking inside as she tried to interpret the meaning.

I sat there, holding my breath and drying my sweaty palms on my formerly white pants.

As I glanced over to my right, I saw Nene looking much as I did, nervous, as her fortuneteller flipped Tarot cards and told her what they meant. She was out of earshot so I didn't hear any of her reading.

As I waited in suspense, my black-haired fortuneteller began her reading, "You will have a long and very prosperous life. You will move very far away from your home, family, and loved ones, across a great body of water. Your life will be most colorful and unconventional." She turned the cup around some more and then continued. "You will explore many paths and walk down many avenues before you find your way. There will be much creative energy. This energy will find a way out, and at some point, you will no longer be able to control the floodgates. One day you will become a painter and a writer of great stories. Places you wish to see in the world, you will see them all. You will direct your life as you see fit, and you will dance your own dance and live your own dream."

She looked up from the cup and gazed at me with her piercing green eyes, as if she was seeing right through me, into the future somehow. She shook her head a bit and looked back into my cup and then back into my eyes. Taking hold of both my cold, clammy hands, which were by now shaking uncontrollably, she leaned in closer and said in hushed tones, "There will be great danger in your life very soon. You must be aware of your surroundings and do not be fearful but act quickly."

As suddenly as she'd picked up my hands, she abruptly let them drop as if they were hot coals, looked at the waitress, and said, "That is all. She can go now."

And just like that, my fortune had been read and I was left wondering how much of it, if any, was real. The last thing she told me was disturbing.

My sister was still getting her cards read. Carolina had been the first one back at the table after having her palm read, and Ruben was still having his tea leaves read.

Carolina wanted to know how it had gone, but I told her I'd rather wait for my sister so I didn't have to repeat myself.

She had been very impressed with her reading. Carolina told me that many of the things the Romani woman said were true, and had just happened or were about to happen. For instance, Carolina was told she would be soon taking a long voyage. Well, her father told her just before she left the house that he was sending Carolina to be a travel companion for her elderly aunt who was going back to Spain. He didn't want the aunt to travel alone so Carolina would accompany her. She would stay with her aunt for a whole month. The predictions had been accurate.

Hearing that only made me feel more nervous and anxious about leaving as soon as possible and getting home safely. Carolina could sense that I was edgy. She asked me again what my tea leaves revealed, and before I had a chance to say anything, my sister showed up and right behind her was Ruben. I didn't even let them sit down before I blurted out, "We have to get home now. I don't want to stay here any longer, and it's getting too late. We're really going to be in trouble for being out so late." It was 5:15 p.m., which wasn't that late if we'd been in town. But we were out in the slums, and it was going to take at least one and a half hours to get back to the park, and then we'd still have to take another bus home.

Nene looked puzzled and said, "What is wrong with you? We should stay a while longer and listen to the music now that we're here. Why do you suddenly want to leave?"

I let it all out and told them briefly about all the good things the woman had said, but the last prediction was the one I was really worried about. That pretty much ended all the jovial conversation.

Ruben said he thought we'd all better listen to the fortuneteller because he was sure they know what they're talking about. His reading was also too accurate to disregard any warning. With that, we got up and headed out the door.

It was beginning to get dark by now. Ruben suggested, "We'd better try to find a taxi to take us back to La Alameda. We can all catch a bus home from there. I don't think we should get on a bus in this neighborhood at this late hour. There are too many people around here that look like they would love to rob some silly kids."

We waited on the corner to see if anything would go by, but there didn't seem to be many taxis in that area. Carolina suggested we go to the other side of the intersection to try to flag a passing cab going in the right direction.

I felt strongly that we should stay put, so I said, "You know, guys, it might be better to wait here, like Ruben said, in case there are some other kids who have taken a taxi to get here. Maybe we can hop in and take it back to town. I'm sure not all these kids came on the bus. How stupid was it that we did? It's not like we were going to the Museum of Anthropology or Chapultepec Park, right? I mean we're in a bad barrio here. I think we should wait a few minutes."

They all looked at me with exasperation, but just then, a cab came speeding up to the corner, and just as I'd figured, four girls hopped out of the cab and started to head into the club. Ruben immediately stuck his head in and asked if the taxi could take us back to town.

I think I said a dozen Hail Marys right there on the spot and all within a split second. "Oh please, God, don't let us get stuck on a scary bus," I thought in silence.

Ruben told us to get in. As I climbed in, my legs instantly turned to jelly, partly from relief and partly from the fear-induced adrenaline rush.

On the way back to La Alameda, we shared all our stories. The only thing I did not repeat was the final sentence, heavy with an ominous warning. I didn't want to tempt fate. Amazingly, we got through our taxi ride unscathed.

So we all figured, great, no problem, we'll take our usual buses home.

Big mistake.

We said goodbye to our friends and went our separate ways. As our buses pulled out into traffic, my sister and I relaxed a bit and kept going over the day. We were rehearsing what we'd say when we got home on the chance that my parents asked any questions.

As we rattled on with our frivolous conversation, the time went by quickly, and before we realized it, we were only a couple of blocks away from our stop. I suddenly heard the voice of my fortuneteller, as if she was sitting right in front of me, shout out, "You're in great danger . . . be aware of your surroundings . . . act quickly." I swear I must have jumped a foot off the bus seat.

My sister looked at me with confusion and said, "What's wrong with you? You look like you saw a ghost or something."

I leaned over to her and whispered, "The Romani woman, my fortuneteller, . . . she just yelled out we're in danger; we need to act quickly." I suddenly felt this very black, cold chill run down my back, and all my blood went straight down to my feet. They felt like lead, and my heart felt like it was close to exploding. I could feel the veins on my neck pulsating and my head beginning to pound. I tried to not focus on the fear, but it was almost impossible.

I quickly looked around the bus; most of the passengers looked pretty harmless. There was a middle-aged lady with her three small children, an old man with a grey beard and a scarf around his neck, and several students who looked like they might be in their twenties heading back to the university.

And then I saw, out of the corner of my eye, a man in the back of the bus with a scruffy-looking beard and a dark-colored jacket with the collar raised up over his neck and a hat pulled down covering some of his face, like he was trying to be invisible. Again I heard her voice, this time whispering, "Be aware of your surroundings . . . act quickly." I told my sister, "Get up, now!" And just then I yelled "Bajan."

The doors opened, and we jumped out for dear life. We crossed the highway just before the light turned green.

I didn't care that cars were still headed in our direction. I had the feeling that I'd rather run through the passing cars and take my chances than find out what that scary man had in mind.

We ran like fools across the street. Cars were rushing by, and we were weaving in and out of the traffic. We had to cross a six-lane highway, three lanes in each direction with a traffic island in the middle. It was crazy, I knew that, but we had no other option. By some miracle, we made it to the other side of the highway. It was still half a block from the corner to the entrance of our apartment. We were going to have to run faster than we'd ever run before, and that's what we did . . . just like two Olympic sprinters, we bolted down the street.

As we're running, I said, "Nene, get your key out and have it ready to open the door."

"Yeah, good idea," she huffed back, all the while fumbling with her purse as she searched for the key. As we ran, I looked back over my shoulder, and to my horror, the man had some-how gotten off the bus, had just made it across the highway, and was running in our direction down the street.

"Don't look back. We're being followed," I warned my sister.

As soon as I saw his face, I felt as though I might throw up. But we just kept running. As we got to our building, we made a sharp right turn up the stairs. My sister had her key out, but her hands were shaking so badly it took the two of us to get the key in the lock. As the door opened, we ran in and immediately turned around and slammed the door shut. We wasted no time in running around the side of the elevator to the stairwell and ran up all six flights of stairs, just on the chance the man would look in the door and try to see on what floor the elevator stopped.

I guess it was the aftermath of sheer fright, but I nonchalantly remarked, "I'm glad we're in pretty good shape since we're used to running up the stairs every day."

"Oh yeah, right," Nene replied. "We're in real good shape, but we're really stupid, aren't we?" And she burst into tears. Her reaction to the fright had been much different from mine. I think I must have been in denial.

I grabbed her hand and kept on running up the stairs just on the far-out chance the man in pursuit had somehow gotten in. I didn't want to chance anything at this point.

In my lame attempt to reassure her, I admitted, "Hey, you weren't stupid all by yourself, you know. I was right next to you the whole time, so we were both really stupid, okay? Stop beating yourself up about it. Let's just be thankful nothing happened."

Nonetheless, we both felt pretty bad about getting chased but also about what it really meant, that we'd been far from truthful with our parents.

By the time we got to our floor and the front door of the apartment, our legs were wobbling a bit, and we were definitely out of breath.

What a terrifying experience. We'd never felt vulnerable before tonight. Something had just shifted in our reality. We no longer felt immune to the big bad world. It was just outside our door. Maybe it had been there all along, and we'd never noticed it before. We were immature and inexperienced . . . roaming around a great big city . . . never thinking about the consequences of our actions . . . until that night.

We were so glad to be opening the front door; we couldn't get in fast enough.

My dad immediately asked why we were so late. He noticed we were out of breath and asked us why. "Well, because we ran all the way home from the bus stop and then ran up the stairs, Dad. I mean, really." We rolled our eyes a bit to emphasize the point and try to bluff our way out of an uncomfortable situation.

He stood there, with his arms crossed, holding a cigarette in his right hand, and looking like he wasn't buying our casual attitude. But he kept quiet and said no more.

My mom had no problem letting us know she was mad at us for being out so late, and she wanted to know why we'd taken so long. We were a couple of Pinocchios by now and, without skipping a beat, said we'd gone across town to the theater to see *Dr. Zhivago*, which was about three hours long and with the long bus ride and taxi ride to get there and back . . .

Then she took one look at my pants and asked, "¿*Qué te paso? Mira que sucios están tus pantalones*." (What happened to you? Your pants are so dirty.)

I told my mom that the bus seats had been really dirty and not to worry; I'd wash them in the morning.

We hurried into our bedroom and closed the door. My sister and I hugged each other tight and held on for a few minutes, wanting to stay in that moment of gratitude and relief.

I had an urge to get on my knees to thank God that we'd made it home. It wasn't worth taking a chance that my mom would walk in and see me on my knees praying, which would have been a dead giveaway that something was wrong, so I prayed silently. I knew God was listening . . . and maybe even the beautiful green-eyed fortuneteller, who had become my guardian angel. I thanked her too.

Nene and I were pretty sober. We got into our pajamas, brushed our teeth, and without much more conversation, went to say good night to our parents. It seemed as though they sensed something had happened, but they didn't press us. They told us to get to bed, get a good rest, and sleep in the next morning.

After I crawled under my warm flannel covers, I lay there quite some time, my mind racing, unable to fall asleep.

The tea leaves had predicted what was going to happen. That was impossible to put out of my mind. And if she had been right about that, I couldn't help but wonder—were her other predictions and forecast about my future also going to be right?

The thin line between truth and deception got blurry that night as reality, drama, fear, remorse, excitement, adventure, honesty, and the supernatural got stirred into the same pot. It left me feeling exhausted.

I hadn't really thought much about this adventure until I sat down to write the story. I have to marvel at the predictions made so long ago.

I did in fact move far away from my home, family, and loved ones, across the big Pacific Ocean to the Hawaiian Islands.

I became a painter and a writer.

My life unfolded in a very colorful and unconventional way that I never would have imagined possible.

I have done a bit of traveling with more on the horizon.

And I have definitely been down many, many long and dusty roads in search of my true path.

If I met my fortuneteller today, I'd have to tell her that, yes, I've learned to dance my own unique dance . . . and that over the years, I've learned to live my own dreams . . . much as she predicted.

Still Waters

OKAY, LET'S BE REAL HONEST with each other. How many of us have been in this situation before? You make friends with people, you open up and trust that everyone is on the same page, never once thinking that you might be the only one on that page.

Yeah? You know exactly what I'm talking about. You don't look past the obvious, or worse yet, you don't even clue in to the obvious.

Well, that's the way it was for me growing up in an aura of trust. I suppose it was my sheltered upbringing that kept me from being as critical of unusual characters as I should have been. By the time I entered college and moved away from home, lifestyles in general were more relaxed, and by relaxed, I mean sex and drugs played a part of that lifestyle, whether you were on that page or not.

One day in 1971, while sitting in my Chinese philosophy class, I met Francisco. Though no alarms went off in my head to tell me that he was in another dimension, I found him intriguing and mysterious. He was different.

Very different and different was good, right?

He spoke no more than a few words for every twenty sentences I spoke. He nodded a lot and tugged on his full black beard.

During the semester, we got to be pretty good friends. One day after class, he invited me over to his house. I thought it would be great to get to know him better; he seemed like a laid-back kind of guy.

We were both big fans of riding bikes wherever we could. He said he didn't live far from campus. I suppose "far from campus" is a relative term. So off we went on our bikes, headed north.

After miles through heavy traffic, near expressways, and up and down more hills than I'd ever been on, we still weren't there.

I had a hard time keeping up. At times I felt like I was going to get sick to my stomach, and I was beginning to regret accepting his invitation. As I felt my legs turning into rubbery versions of my once-hard, muscled legs, I began to panic. I wondered if I'd be able to ride my bike all the way back home. I shook off the worry and told myself that as long as I could see him off in the distance, I'd be okay. After a couple more miles, we finally rounded the corner to his street in a suburban neighborhood.

The house he was renting was large for one person. He said he liked living alone, as he didn't want to be distracted from his studies. Plus, he added, it helped him in other aspects of his life.

Being curious by nature, of course I asked him what those other aspects might be.

First, he told me he was a vegetarian. I thought that was pretty cool. In the early seventies, being a vegetarian was not as mainstream as it is now. I didn't have any friends who were vegetarian. And a funny thing was that within three years I would convert to a vegetarian way of life. Who knew?

The second benefit to living alone was that he was celibate, so it simplified his life. Being celibate at a time when free love, self-expression, and letting it all hang out was more the norm, for me, sounded a bit Puritanical if not radical. It was this most unusual vow that I found fascinating, especially for an attractive, well-built, twenty-year-old male.

What came to my mind, selfishly of course, was "Great, I can have a friend who is male without having to worry about sex getting in the way of friendship or even being a topic of conversation." He could be a friend with no complications, worries, or games. Those types of friends were very hard to find on campus. It felt like a good thing, and I jumped right in.

Though he rode his bike to campus every day, he had a car that he used only when he needed to buy groceries. On one occasion he mentioned after class that he was going to the store on Saturday, if I wanted a ride. Well, sure I did. I didn't have a car, and the student shuttle bus service didn't pass by any major grocery stores, so you pretty much had to hitch a ride or know someone with a car and beg.

Francisco drove up to my house on Saturday morning, I got into his yellow Mercury sedan and didn't notice anything unusual. I just hopped in, and off we went.

He took me to a big supermarket on the north side of town. I rarely ventured that far north, travelling mostly within the shuttle bus routes. Usually I shopped at a more expensive health food co-op, not because I was a health nut but because it was on the bus route. On occasion, if I had to travel further, I'd stand out on Enfield Road where I lived and hitch a ride. When I had to get to the library on a weekend or on a day the buses weren't running, I usually walked or rode my bike to campus, up and down many hills. The miles-long walk home at night was a bit grueling.

Never a big fan of hitchhiking, I did it only when necessary. I tried to avoid situations like that, but life's not always easy to control, is it? I'd already had several opportunities to use my creative talents in hitching a ride back home. And it was a talent I didn't care to summon very often.

Francisco and I drove up to the supermarket, and he parked his cumbersome Mercury. I got out of the car, ran to grab a shopping cart, and headed in the store to start shopping, leaving Francisco behind. As I started down the fresh produce aisle, Francisco had caught up to me and was standing right next to me. It was only then that I noticed he was wearing a funky, well-worn, and faded blue terry cloth bathrobe and a pair of house slippers (which explained why I hadn't heard him sneak up on me). I was a bit surprised or better yet, shocked. A bathrobe? I must have been distracted during our car ride with conversation or perhaps his charming smile to not have noticed his wardrobe before that moment, but I hadn't. I couldn't believe that anyone would go to a big supermarket wearing a bathrobe and house slippers. This was one eccentric friend I'd made.

I turned to Francisco and said, "A bathrobe, Paco, really? To the grocery store? What are you wearing under your bathrobe? No, never mind, I really don't want to know. Do you realize what you might look like to other people? Do you want to get arrested? Is that it? Because if you do, you need to make sure you give me your car keys so I can drive myself home."

"No, I don't want to get arrested, and I'm not going to get arrested. I was way too comfortable to change, and it's Saturday, so I'm relaxing in my Saturday-morning clothes." Had he just told me he was too comfortable to change? I mean, what planet was he from? He was odd. No doubt about it. The real issue for me was his odd behavior and how it affected me . . . was it anything I needed to worry about? I mulled that over a few times in my mind as I pushed my cart through the produce aisle and on to the milk, eggs, and cheese aisle.

Other than the outfit, everything else Francisco did and said seemed perfectly coherent and normal. I took stock of his method of shopping. He looked at all the food he was buying carefully, checked out all the ingredients, and did some price comparisons. I figured if he was sane enough to be a good shopper, then he must have all his shopping carts in a row, so no worries.

I, on the other hand, dressed like a "normal" person when I went grocery shopping, but I usually went straight for the packages that had more visual appeal and artistic designs on the labels, even if they were more expensive than the other store brands. So what did that say about me? I wondered who was really nuts.

Paco kept his bathrobe closed the whole time in the store and didn't talk much the rest of the time we shopped.

I decided to leave it to my imagination what he might or might not be wearing under the bathrobe.

We got to my four-plex and he helped me up the stairs with my groceries. I insisted I didn't want or need any help carrying up my groceries, but he helped me anyway. I suppose that was nice of him to do. As Paco was walking out the front door, he mentioned casually that he was driving to the Valley to see his parents the following weekend and if I wanted a ride, he'd drop me off at my house and pick me up when he headed back to Austin. Easter break was coming up, and I knew this would be the only way for me to get home.

I jumped at the chance, bathrobe or no bathrobe; I'd hitch a ride with Paco. Without any hesitation, I said, "Sure, that would be great. Only thing is I don't have any extra cash to contribute for gas money, so I understand if you'd rather not let me bum a ride off you."

As Paco walked out the front door, he looked back and said, "I don't need any money, so don't worry about it. I'll drop you off at your house and pick you up on the way out of the Valley."

Wow, that sounded like a win/win for me. I was so excited. I was going to get to see my mom and dad and eat my mom's cooking. All the homemade flour tortillas and beans I could eat . . . yum. That thought put a smile on my face and a bit of drool down my chin, as my mind lingered on the soft, plump, and hot buttery tortillas I'd soon have in my mouth.

My mom never put a limit on how many I could eat. She was so cool about that. I remember grabbing six flour tortillas, one after another, just as soon as they came off her cast iron *comal* (griddle) and slathering Falfurrias butter all over them. God, they were good. No . . . they were great.

Three weeks before my trip home, I had picked up a stray dog on campus. I couldn't help myself. She was scared and hungry, and I did what I had to do, picked her up and carried her home. I named her Good Karma because I really felt like it had been a bit of good karma to find her. She was sweet and gentle, and I knew she'd be a faithful companion. When I got her home from campus that first night, it was one of the most beautiful sunsets I'd seen—peach, pink, and yellow all swirled together in vibrant tones . . . an unforgettable and electric sunset—so I chose Sunset as her last name. I tied on the only piece of jewelry I owned, a strip of brown leather with a small turquoise pendant around her neck, and that became her dog collar. I thought she looked like a cool hippie dog.

The day came to go back home for a visit. I took Karma and my backpack with a few clothes and waited in the driveway for my ride.

Paco finally showed up in a white sleeveless undershirt, blue pinstriped Bermuda shorts, and bare feet, I figured, he must be wearing another version of his comfort clothes. He gave me a big toothy smile, as always. He had very full lips, a huge smile that he handed out freely, and dark-brown glossy eyes beneath his granny glasses. I threw my backpack in the trunk of the car and let Karma have one last potty break before climbing aboard the Paco Train.

We were on our way south to the Rio Grande Valley, and it was a long drive. By nightfall, we had reached King Ranch, which was the largest privately owned ranch in the country at the time. As we reached the outskirts of town before entering the ranch, there were signs everywhere saying there were no gas stations, diners, or anything for that matter until you got to the other side of the ranch. So if you needed gas, food, a bathroom break, tire pressure check, oil check, or anything else, you needed to go back into town and do your business before entering the ranch.

Paco said we were fine and we didn't need anything, so we just drove right through the last town and entered the remote ranchland. There are no lights of any kind anywhere on that stretch of road. The only things that are bright are the stars above you and the headlights of your car. There is so little traffic in the ranch at night that it is unlikely you'd ever see a passing car or headlights coming toward you from the opposite direction. As we drove further and further along the highway, we also drove deeper and deeper into an all-consuming darkness. It was a bit spooky driving through the King Ranch at night. It was desolate. I'd never been through the ranch at night, so my nerves were a bit rattled.

To pass the time, I asked Paco about his mid-term assignment. We'd turned them in to our philosophy professor before we left. We both felt confident in our work, but you never knew with this professor. Half the time I couldn't understand a word he said because his accent was so heavy, and most of the class didn't know what was going on. I relied solely on my books and the little bit of help I got from the teaching assistant.

Somehow Francisco and I managed to drive about halfway through the ranch before we felt a relaxed and mellow mood emerge in us both.

Just as I was letting my guard down, the yellow Mercury began to sound ill, as if it had whooping cough, and began to lunge forward as if it was trying to cough up something stuck in the engine or maybe the carburetor. All I heard Paco say was "Hmm," and he started to stroke his beard as if that was going to magically help him figure out what the hell was happening to his car.

He veered off the highway and onto the right-hand shoulder. And as if the car had somehow divined it was safely off the highway, it quietly stopped dead in its tracks. Just like that. No more wheezing, coughing, or gagging; officially dead in our world and perhaps alive in some parallel universe.

I'm embarrassed to admit this, but I started to get mad at Paco. He apparently wasn't the least bit mechanically inclined. I knew it was a stereotypical way of looking at Paco, but I had imagined that knowing how to fix cars was something men were supposed to learn in a high school auto mechanics class. I mean, as a woman, I knew society made it pretty darn clear that there were certain things we women were expected to know how to do too, some of which we may have learned in a high school home economics class. Nonetheless, there we were, stranded in that godforsaken King Ranch, in the middle of the night. I tried as best I could to shake off the negative thoughts, but . . .

Bottom line, we were stuck out in the middle of nowhere with no idea of how to get out of the dark that instantly swallowed us up once the car lights went out. Stuck out on King Ranch was no joke. There were lots of wild animals that roamed around after dark; some, such as a wild boar, might even want to charge you.

Then I turned the blame onto me, getting mad at myself for being so quick to jump at the chance to get out of town to see my parents. I started to second-guess myself, like maybe I didn't know Paco well enough to take a long trip alone with him, or that just because it was a free ride didn't mean I had to take it.

Everything was a little more complicated having Karma with me; I'd have to hitch a ride for two. I was always uncomfortable having to hitchhike, let alone in the middle of King Ranch at night. Then I told myself how unproductive my train of thought was because it was unlikely we'd even see a passing car all night long, so it was doubtful I'd be hitching any time soon. No, we were stranded, and we'd just have to make the best of it. There were no cell phones back then. There was no one we could call for help, no one that is, other than the universe.

And that's exactly what I started to do, call out to the universe in my own way. I stepped out of the car, took Karma with me, and started to walk. And as I walked, I paused to look up at the night sky. It was a cool spring night, bordering on chilly, and the sky was littered with shining, twinkling orbs of light, some blinking, some steady, stars so bright they

almost looked fake. Knowing so many stars, planets, and gal-
axies were always out there, even if we couldn't see them in
daylight hours, left me feeling tiny and insignificant.

Once my eyes were adjusted to total darkness, I saw shooting stars, one right after another. The night, in all its darkness,
was suddenly . . . peaceful, welcoming, and even protective. I
felt like a speck in an infinite universe. However, my smallness
was at peace. Amid the noises of the night, I could've heard a
pin drop. In a moment of stillness, I realized being stuck out
here all night might not be such a bad thing after all.

And just like that, once I'd made peace with my circum-
stances, the universe made a concession. Far off in the distance, a dot of light was headed in our direction. As the light
got larger, I realized that it was definitely a car.

I walked back to the car and saw that Paco had fallen
asleep. "Wake up. There's a car coming toward us. Let's see if
it'll stop."

"Huh? A car? Ha, no way. I told you not to worry, didn't
I?" he said.

"Well, I don't exactly remember you saying much more
than 'hmm,' but, whatever. I don't really care. I just want the
car to stop."

As soon as it appeared to get closer, we stepped out to the
edge of the highway and started to wave for the car to stop.
It was actually an old, rusty, red Ford pickup truck with a
cowboy behind the wheel, maybe in his mid-fifties, with a
shotgun mounted on a gun rack by the back window. "Oh
great, a gun rack," I mumbled under my breath. I was never
fond of guns.

"Hi there," Paco said. "My car seems to have died. Do
you think we could hitch a ride to the gas station on the
other side of the ranch?"

"Sure you ain't outta gas?" the cowboy questioned.

"No, I'm sure. We had three-quarters of a tank when we started through the ranch. It's probably the carburetor or spark plugs," Paco answered, sounding like he actually knew something about cars when he really didn't.

"All right then, kids, get in the truck," the cowboy offered.

I walked up closer to the truck to let him see I had Karma in my arms. "Can she come in the truck too, because if not, I'll ride in the bed of the truck with her if you want," I said in the most pathetic voice I could muster.

He gave me a big smile and then said, "There's plenty of room for y'all three. Hop in."

That was nice of him, I thought. Paco threw our backpacks in the bed of the truck, I got in with Karma, and then he climbed in. I got Karma to sit on the floorboards to give us more room. Then we were off.

After introducing ourselves, he told us his name was Mack McKenny, and it was lucky for us he'd been late leaving Dimebox, which is why he was driving through the ranch so late.

"You know you probably won't be able to find a ride at the gas station, but at least there's a pay phone, and you can let your folks know your car broke down and you need a ride home."

I knew Mack was just trying to be helpful, but his comments dampened my spirits. We didn't say too much after that. He spent the rest of the time fiddling with the radio trying to pick up a station to no avail.

The last part of the ride through the ranch flew by rather quickly. I suppose I was just so glad to be on the other side I hadn't taken notice of anything.

But as we approached the gas station, I saw a small, white four-door sedan and a person putting gas in the car. The wheels started to turn in my head. I certainly didn't feel like one of the three musketeers right then; no "one for all and all for one" for me. I figured that Paco would probably be his spacey self and I'd end up having to find a ride home for Karma and me. Besides, it was a small car, and if they were even going my way, I'd still have to figure out where to put Karma.

Mack pulled into the station. He let us grab our backpacks and said goodbye. We yelled out, as he pulled away, "Thanks, Mack. It was mighty nice of you to stop." He just tipped his hat and drove off into the night.

"Well, Paco, what do you suggest we do?" I was really hoping he was going to tell me to see if I could hitch a ride with the folks in the white sedan.

"Hmm" was about all that rolled out of his mouth.

"Hmm? That's it? No ideas how we're going to get home?" I asked feeling rather frustrated by this time.

"Well, I'm going to call my dad and see if he can come get us," Paco responded. "Of course, assuming he can do it, that'll be at least two hours before he gets here, another two hours to get you home, and then another hour and a half before I'm home. So that's what I'm going to do. How's that sound?"

"Well, I've got Karma, and I don't think I want to hang around for two hours for your dad to maybe pick us up. I'm going to ask the people in that car over there for a ride, okay? If they say yes, I'm going to get going. I'll take a bus back to Austin."

I hurried over to the white car, introduced myself, and asked the short stocky guy who was putting gas in the car if by chance they were headed to Brownsville and if so, if I could get a ride since our car had broken down.

He told me that they were all heading home to Brownsville and they'd make room for one more. It was obvious to me that the universe had, once again, come to my aid. Oh man, was I relieved, yet I had a twinge of guilt leaving Paco there at the station.

By the time I got back to Paco to tell him I had a ride home, he'd already called his dad and he was on his way. Paco assured me it was fine to leave without him. They planned to find a motel and stay overnight so they could get the car towed the following day. He told me his offer was still on to pick me up on the way back to Austin and I didn't need to take a bus. I thought about it and realized I wouldn't be able to take Karma on the bus anyway so, sure, I told him he could pick me up.

As I walked with Karma toward our ride, I turned to say bye to Paco, but he'd already gone inside the convenience store. I could see him picking up the sodas and looking at them closely, probably checking all the ingredients and doing a quick price comparison.

"Okay, guys, I'm here. Thanks again for letting me bum a ride. We got stranded in the middle of the ranch, and if it hadn't been for that cowboy who happened to drive by and give us a ride, well, we'd still be out there in the dark with all the coyotes," I offered as part of my introduction.

"Hey, we're glad to help out a *chica* (girl) from Brownsville. Squeeze in," the stocky guy said to me. "*Oyes vatos* (guys), move over, man. Make room for the cute girl," he told the passengers in the back seat and then back to me, "I think your dog will have to ride on your lap or maybe on Felipe's head like a hood ornament if it's too crowded," he said.

I managed to squeeze Karma and myself into the backseat. There I was, my body glued next to a total stranger. It felt weird. I managed to get Karma to lie on my lap, stretched out facing the back of the driver's seat.

Once I had a second to look around, the persons riding up front were both guys, students by the look of them, maybe around their early twenties. I gathered from the conversation that the driver was named Memito and the person on the passenger side, who had given me the ride, was Mario.

The three passengers in the back were all guys too, a fact I hadn't noticed at first. Two of the guys were rather chunky looking, or maybe they were muscular. It was hard to tell, or maybe the car was just too small. The third person was slender, which was a good thing since they were already crammed into that tiny backseat before I got in with Karma, and now we were stuffed like a fat tamale popping out of its cornhusk wrapper. Turns out they were all business majors at the University of Texas at Austin, and they were glad to hear I was an English major at UT, so it was all in the family, "Hook 'em Horns," they chanted in unison.

My legs, feet, and arms were cramping from being crammed in so tight. I couldn't help but feel sorry for the guys in the backseat, whose names I had learned were Ricky, Carlos, and Felipe. Felipe was practically an extension of my own body as we were sitting that close. They made a sacrifice letting us both jump on board. I got the phone numbers for their dorm rooms and promised to bring them back some of my mom's homemade flour tortillas. They were happy with that arrangement.

The remainder of the ride home was uneventful. I fell asleep the rest of the way home. The next thing I knew, we were pulling up in front of my house. We made a bit of a ruckus getting out of the car, and I noticed that my dad had gotten up and turned the porch light on to see who was outside.

I had wanted to surprise my parents, and that's what I did. Once my dad saw me standing outside the car, he came out to see who all the guys were. By reading his facial expressions, I was pretty certain he was not pleased to see me in a car full of men. After I made all the introductions, I told my dad how kind they were to give me a ride home after our car had broken down in the middle of King Ranch. He pulled out a twenty-dollar bill from his wallet and said he hoped it helped with the gas money. Memito shook my dad's hand and thanked him for the money, saying it would help them with their trip back to Austin. I waved goodbye and of course gave them the ol' Hook 'em Horns traditional hand gesture as they drove off.

My parents were happy to see me; they almost overlooked the fact that I had just brought a dog into the house. We'd had a Chihuahua when we were growing up. After Princess had died, they didn't want any more dogs in the house. So Karma's appearance opened up a can of worms in the middle of the night. Oh well, I'd had my first confrontation with my parents, and I wasn't home even a half-hour.

After a couple of days, they made peace with my Karma and allowed her in the house. My dad made some kind of surly remark about her hippie collar. The rest of my stay was happy with no conflicts whatsoever. I slept, ate, hung out with my mom, and did nothing extraordinary . . . it was perfect.

Before I left, my mom made me a huge stack of flour tortillas, enough for me to share with the guys who'd given me a ride home, as I'd promised.

The Sunday I was scheduled to return to Austin finally arrived, and Paco came by to pick me up. I threw my backpack in the trunk along with a large brown paper grocery bag filled three-fourths of the way with pinto beans, which they sold loose by the pound at a local grocery store. They were really cheap that way, and they were, after all, my staple and main source of protein.

I said my tearful goodbyes to my parents and saw them standing at the end of our sidewalk, waving goodbye, as we drove off. Seeing them again reminded me of how much I missed them both. It also made me aware that I wasn't a child anymore—conscious of the passage of time; of the inevitable time I'd be alone, on my own, making my way through life, whatever it would bring; of the possibility that it could be the last time I'd see my parents standing there at the end of our sidewalk, waving goodbye to their youngest. We were all getting older, especially my dad who was about twelve years older than my mom. I felt so melancholy, so isolated, even though there was another person in the car and of course Karma, who was resting on the back seat.

I turned to Paco and said, "I'm not sure that leaving the nest is all that it's cracked up to be. I mean, who really wants to leave safety? Security? Unconditional love? Who? Do you know anyone?"

He didn't respond, other than mumbling, "Hmmm," and kept his eyes on the road.

I kept quiet.

During the ride, I noticed how nicely Paco's car sounded, and to break the ice a bit, I commented on that, thinking it was a nice thing to say. He started to laugh and said it was ironic that I was saying something positive about something that had been such a bummer for me before. He then confided that when his dad finally showed up at the gas station, it was not a happy reunion. "Honestly, I had no clue of how to take care of a car. Apparently, I never took care of the car. I never took it in for the required maintenance checkups, ever, which is why the car fell apart. It ended up staying with the mechanic for several days and cost a small fortune to fix," he said. According to Paco, his dad had gotten upset with him because he was irresponsible, ungrateful, immature, careless, and thoughtless, and all sorts of other bad things. Paco's reaction seemed strangely calm. I think if my dad had said all those things about me, I would have been crying while reliving the moment.

I told Paco I was truly sorry it had been so hard on him. I suddenly felt very tired, closed my eyes, and fell into a deep sleep.

If you've ever driven out of the Rio Grande Valley, you've likely seen a US Border Patrol checkpoint somewhere before you entered King Ranch. The agents were always on the lookout for illegal aliens and I suppose any potential drug smuggling. I never gave its presence much thought. You'd slow down at the guard station, a Border Patrol agent would walk up to your car, look in, and ask if you were a US citizen. If you weren't a US citizen, you had to have some proof of identification, your visa, passport, or proof of legal entry into the United States. However, if you were a US citizen, you never had to worry about it. I never carried any proof of citizenship, ever. I suspect that rules may have toughened up more now, and I imagine there is still some sort of checkpoint somewhere.

In the middle of my deep sleep, I felt the car slow down and woke up, a bit blurry-eyed and sweaty. I had my window rolled all the way down, but it was only hot air blowing in.

A Border Patrol agent appeared to be waving us to go on by, at least that's what Paco said. It seemed odd because I thought you always had to stop, no matter what. So we kept on going right through the checkpoint. We hadn't gotten more than a few hundred feet when all of a sudden, a Border Patrol car came speeding up to us with a light flashing, motioning us to pull the vehicle over.

Oh man, what had we done? You don't mess with a Border Patrol agent, even if you are a US citizen.

Paco slowly made it safely over to the right shoulder of the road. As the officer approached the car, he asked why we didn't stop at the checkpoint. Paco put on the most repentant and innocent sounding voice and said, "I'm so sorry, Officer. Did we do something wrong? Weren't you telling us to drive on through?"

I'm over here thinking, "We? We?" I would've stopped. I would never pass a Border Patrol station without coming to a full stop. Was he crazy?

The agent said he wasn't flagging us to go through; he was flagging us to pull over to the side, as they were checking all the cars. And by the way, were we US citizens? Well we both chimed in yes, of course we were.

Just then, my sweet like Karma went over to the window and stuck her head out by the officer and started wagging her tail.

The agent said to Paco, "Your dog?"

"No, it's my friend's," and he pointed to me.

I stupidly and nervously said, "Yep, she's mine, a stray dog I found on campus." "Shut up!" I said to myself. Don't act nervous and don't talk. I had nothing to be nervous about, but you hear stories about being pulled over, and after all I was Mexican American, born in Texas of course, but I'd heard plenty of horror stories growing up, and I didn't have any ID on me other than a driver's license and my student ID.

The officer asked us where we were headed and Paco told him we were going back to Austin after our spring break, and then, as he looked at Karma wagging her tail, he grinned and told us, "Go on ahead. Be careful, and remember to always stop at the checkpoint, no driving through. Ya hear me?"

"Yes, sir, absolutely, will do," Paco responded with the most sincere voice he could muster.

Whew, that was it. We drove back to Austin, not talking much, without the radio—in silence.

I wasn't quite sure what my spring break had been about. I was in a rush to go see my family but so many things about the trip, in general, had been unnerving.

We finally made it back to Austin, and I was in front of my four-plex. I was so happy to be back.

"Thanks for the ride, Paco. You know how much I appreciated it, right?" I said.

"Yeah, I'm glad you had a good time with your folks. Can't say I had much fun. Not even sure what made me want to go back home. Anyway, I did have a couple of friends to see, but that was it. Let's get your stuff out of the trunk."

I got Karma and my bag of flour tortillas out of the car and went around to the trunk. As Paco opened the trunk, I got out my backpack and reached for the brown-paper grocery bag with my beans. When I picked up the bag of beans, it was awfully light.

I said, "Hey, what happened to my beans?" I opened the bag and looked in. To my utter horror, shock, surprise . . . I don't know, I could go on and on, describing how I felt the moment I opened up Paco's grocery bag instead of mine.

He calmly said, "You got the wrong bag there, girl." He reached over, closed it up, and pulled out my bag of beans.

While he'd been in the Valley, he'd gone shopping too, only he'd bought what looked like to me a year or two's supply of pot. Yeah, POT, no joke. All the buds you could possibly smoke for a long, long time.

I just about passed out when I realized that the Border Patrol agent, for whatever reason, chose to let us go without searching the car, which is what they would have done had we pulled over the first time. Had they searched the car, I'd have been in as much trouble as Paco, even though I had no clue what he was doing. I felt like such an idiot. How could I have been so blind to his super-mellow moods? His far away looks? I just thought he was introspective, but maybe that was the pot and not his deep thoughts or the deep thoughts he had when he was smoking pot. Whichever it was, I was in shock. And speechless. I couldn't believe Paco had taken that much pot in the trunk of his car, like it was beans or toilet paper or canned soup. I had no idea he even smoked pot, let alone was buying that much pot. For all I knew he was a dealer. I really had no clue, and I didn't want to know either.

Without saying another word, I turned around and grabbed all my stuff and headed to the door. He offered to help, but I said, "Absolutely not. Goodbye."

And that was that. I never sat by him in class again, and we lost track of each other after our philosophy class ended.

When I began to write about this memory, I had to wonder why I wanted to share it in the form of a story. It was hard to write about. But I decided that it was only fair to you to know about some of the less pleasant things that happened to me too. It made me think about the times when I didn't process enough information about people, taking everything at face value.

As I got older, maybe even a bit wiser, I learned through many painful twists and turns in my life that face value was never enough. I also needed to function with all my burners on. I couldn't rely on just one element to determine what I felt or believed in. What I had to learn to do was listen and trust my intuition. My intuition was most often present, yet most often ignored by me.

If you are as lucky as I am—having grown up in a family that loved you and protected you unconditionally—the downside might be that you became too trusting. And as life, or the universe, always seems to have a way of balancing things out, my innocence was tested and tumbled many,

many times. Along the way, I received important lessons that had to be learned the hard way.

I was grateful to see other aspects to Paco's life so I was better able to choose my own path. I learned what the old adage "still waters run deep" was about. Some people live in the deepest of waters, the deep blue.

I was thankful to have had a kind Border Patrol agent who was having a good day and chose to give us a stern warning, rather than do a vehicle search.

I was grateful for the good karma that my own Good Karma Sunset brought to us when she sweetly wagged her tail at the Border Patrol agent and maybe, just maybe, melted his heart enough to let us go on our way.

Life's never one dimensional, is it? Always the good with the bad, the happy with the sad, the rich with the lean . . . and in this case, with my life in particular, it has always been the eye-opening experiences with the lessons learned. I suppose I wouldn't have wanted it any other way. Would you?

Sweet Sixteen

M Y DAD WAS ALWAYS FULL OF SURPRISES. Just when you thought he'd forgotten something important, he'd make some grand gesture to let you know he indeed remembered.

I'm sure my dad was not much different from most dads in the fifties and sixties. They were more reserved back then. Though he may not have been one of those mushy types, I always knew how much he loved me. It was obvious in so many ways, just not in a literal way where you heard him say the words.

His upbringing was different from ours. His father was very strict and not outwardly affectionate with the children. His mother was a beautiful woman who was very loving and gentle. Everyone who knew her said so. I never got a chance to meet my grandmother because she died before I was born. My grandfather, I saw only once, that I remember, and it was towards the end of his life. I was still quite young and don't recall many details about our visit, other than he frightened me. He was hard of hearing and was getting a little senile, so he didn't know whose child I was.

After my grandfather died, my dad's sisters and brothers looked to him for guidance and financial help as he was the oldest in the family. He was constantly being pulled in many directions. As a child, I never knew what my dad went through. He would never have let his children see any strain he had in his life. He may have discussed things with my mom, but then again, maybe not.

That's what he'd always done in our lives, sheltered us from things he didn't want us to worry about or could do nothing about.

On one of those great summer days, when I was on vacation in Mexico City, visiting my dad who had been working there for a year and a half, he asked me to go with him to town. He had an errand to run at the bank and wanted company. I was always ready to go anywhere he wanted to take me.

He was driving a compact car at the time. Back home, my dad always chose bigger cars, like a Mercury; he felt they were safer, and we needed the room. But in Mexico City, he felt smaller cars were easier to maneuver in the crazy and congested city.

After weaving in and out of thunderous traffic, I could see he was right. He made it to the Hotel del Prado where he wanted us to have lunch. I can't even remember what he did with his car, but I suppose the doorman at the hotel took care of it. Actually I can't imagine where a person could even park a car there. I don't remember there being any parking garages or many cars parked in the streets, for that matter, but maybe I never noticed. I was always too busy looking up at the old buildings with all the Gothic details, such as the gargoyles. I loved walking in the downtown area; architecture fascinated me then and still does.

In the heart of the city, buildings were ancient and

ornately carved from volcanic stone. The churches and cathedrals mesmerized me, and I was always more interested in the architecture than in the landscape. To wander through some of the cathedrals that were built in the 1500s and gaze at the gold-encrusted altars was impressive, and I never forgot the images. As you entered some of the cathedrals and old churches in the city, you actually had to step down a foot or so below street level. The city was originally built on top of a lakebed, and parts of the city were—and still are—slowing sinking, like Venice, I suppose. After the Spanish invaded Mexico, they built directly over an ancient Aztec city built in the 1300s.

I think my dad took us into the heart of the city to let us experience the magnitude of everything around us—the incredible architecture, the sea of humanity that crowded *avenidas* (avenues), the art expressed in statues and fountains, and the many public government buildings that featured murals by famous Mexican artists. I feel it was his way of telling us how much he loved us and hoped our vision of the world was larger than his had been when he was young. Papi wanted us to have a sophisticated appreciation of life and art in all its forms. That he succeeded was undeniable.

It was just another one of his legacies.

The Hotel del Prado had enormous murals that were painted by the Mexican artist Diego Rivera. I know my dad got a kick out of seeing my reaction every time I saw them. The paintings were massive, and I couldn't understand how anyone could manage to paint on such a large surface and make sense. It was life altering for me to see so much beauty. I could feel my nerves tingle with energy and inspiration. My eyes recorded what they saw and made notes of it somewhere in my mind as proof that there was a higher purpose to life . . . more than just being born, living a mundane life, and then dying. It all meant there had to be much, much more.

After lunch, my dad and I took a walk down Madero Street. That was a bit unusual because my dad didn't do much strolling. He usually had places to go and things to do, so window-shopping was not on his agenda. But that is exactly what we did. The area was known for its fine jewelry stores. As we drew closer to the Zócalo, the main square in the city that was lined on one side by jewelry stores, he slowed down his pace, and we began to do some serious browsing.

He'd point at something and ask me for my opinion. And if I commented on how nice something was, he'd want me to point it out to him. Then he'd say, "*¿Te lo compro?*" (Shall I buy it for you?) And I'd start back-pedaling a bit and say, "No, I just think it's pretty. I don't want it." He'd do that to me anytime I showed favor to a piece of jewelry. This happened in every store window we looked at, and there were quite a few.

My dad held my hand from time to time as we walked and always held onto me whenever we crossed a street. I remember thinking about how polished he looked. He had decided to wear a black turtleneck sweater with his black suit and a black beret. With the panache of a Parisian, he was living his dream. And that was good, and I think that was what he was showing me what to do.

As we wandered past the gold stores, my eyes began to get bigger and bigger. I had no idea I'd be so drawn to gold jewelry, but there we were in front of some gorgeous window displays with ornate gold crosses on thick chains and jewelry dripping with rubies, sapphires, and diamonds. I think I might've accidentally drooled.

One ring suddenly said, "I belong to you, little girl. Take me home." I pointed to the gold ring in the window that had a small white pearl in the center and was surrounded with tiny turquoise beads. Its shape was somewhat like a four-pointed star. I'm not exactly sure what it was about the ring that made me want it, but whatever it was, I had fallen in love with my first piece of real jewelry. The ring was completely different from anything else we'd seen. It was elegant and simple. The combination of bright gold and turquoise gave it an exotic Egyptian flavor. I hadn't seen a single other ring like it.

Naturally, my dad took me by the hand and said once again, "*¿Te lo compro?*" and this time I shyly nodded my head yes. He took me in the store. We had the old proprietor with a white handlebar mustache pull it from the window display. The man said to me, "*Este es mi favorito diseño que es muy diferente a los demás. Escogiste bien, niña.*" (This is my favorite design, which is very different from all the rest. You have chosen well, little girl.)

He handed the ring to my dad who placed it on my left hand's ring finger, and lucky for me, it was a perfect fit.

And then he looked at me and said, "*Feliz Cumpleaños mi Patita. Mira que mujercita te has puesto, ya tienes los diez y seis años. . . . ¿Imposible, cómo pudo suceder eso?*" he half mumbled to himself. (Happy birthday, my little Patita. Look at what a young lady you have become, and you're now sixteen years old. Impossible. How could that have happened?) I sensed a bit of melancholy in his voice. Maybe it was the bittersweet feeling a father has when he sees his baby grow up right before his eyes and draw closer to leaving a protective nest.

Whatever reason for his sadness, I felt a little of it too . . . and I suppose part of me knew, at sixteen, the harsh reality of growing up. Whether I wanted it or not, independence was not far off. Part of me always wanted to remain a little girl under the protection of her parents, but I knew that wasn't how reality worked and there would come a time when all I wanted to do was to leave home. Until that day, I'd play the role of baby; it felt like a secure and warm place to be.

When we got home, my aunt, Tía Nile, and cousin, Alicia, there for a two-week visit, greeted us at the door. Tía Nile was Papi's youngest sister and a dead ringer for my dad.

Our apartment had a third bedroom off the kitchen that had most often been used as a maid's quarters. However, since my mom had teenagers around to help her, we never used a maid. That room became our guest quarters.

As soon as I gave my aunt and cousin a hug, I showed my mom the beautiful ring Papi had bought me. She was thrilled that I'd picked out such a unique piece. She thought it went well with my eclectic style. My mom suggested we celebrate my birthday the following day, as my aunt and cousin were tired from the long bus ride from Nuevo Laredo to Mexico City.

That was totally fine with me; my day already felt complete and whole.

The following morning came too quickly, as we'd stayed up late visiting with my aunt and cousin. Though Tía Nile kept nodding off, Alicia was able to stay wide-awake. She was about eight years older than me, so the gap wasn't that big. Alicia had a sharp wit and was gifted in telling stories and jokes; she was always making us laugh. She had inherited that talent from her mother, who was also a natural storyteller, a trait I always admired. By the time I finally went to bed, my face hurt so much from all the laughing we'd done I had to take a couple of aspirins just so I could fall asleep.

We didn't do much that day, other than let my aunt and cousin catch up from the bus ride. Besides, my dad was taking us out to dinner.

That afternoon I got as dressed up as I could. I put on one of the new dresses my mom had made me for the upcoming school year. She had frowned at my bringing it along. She thought I should save it for school, but I wanted something new to wear when we went to see my dad, and this was the perfect time to pull it out. It was a double-breasted, white linen coatdress with brushed gold-colored buttons.

STANDING OUTSIDE THE FANCY RESTAURANT WHERE
I CELEBRATED MY SIXTEENTH BIRTHDAY WITH
(LEFT TO RIGHT) MAMI, PAPI, ME, AND MY AUNT, NILE.

With all the city traffic, it took us an hour and a half to arrive at the restaurant. I knew this was a fancy restaurant because it had international cuisine and there was a man playing a grand piano for atmosphere. Having never been to a restaurant where there was a grand piano, I was duly impressed. And I'm sure we had a great meal. I just don't remember what it was because the dessert topped it all.

As we sat there, I noticed my dad was telling our waiter something, but I had no idea what. After the man left, a few moments went by, and then the pianist began playing "Happy birthday to you . . ." I looked around to see who they were playing for, and out came our waiter holding a big platter with a cake that had a meringue topping and birthday candles. He brought me the cake so I could blow out the candles. Everyone in the restaurant was singing and clapping . . . I was definitely surprised. My dad motioned for me to blow out the candles.

Though it was my birthday dinner, I never expected anything like that from my dad. From my mom, it wouldn't have surprised me, but my dad? Yeah, it was a surprise. It was the kind of mushy thing I'd expect from my mom. But this was all my dad's idea.

I was so touched with Papi's expression of love that I started to cry. My mom, sister, aunt, and cousin all started to cry too. My dad looked a bit embarrassed by his clan of overly emotional ladies.

When the waiter sliced my cake, I saw it wasn't your average cake. It was filled with ice cream. The waiter told me it was called baked Alaska. I had never seen anything like it before and I have never seen it since my sixteenth birthday celebration.

As I said before, my dad was a man of few emotional words, but on occasion he made grand gestures. And on my sixteenth birthday, he made damn sure I had no doubt about how much he loved me then and how much he would always love me, whether he could say it with the words "I love you" or not.

I never doubted my father's love for me, and I know he felt the same way about me, whether I could say the words or not. I was then and still am very much my father's daughter.

Ninetieth

She was born in 1920, and in January she would hit a milestone.

The only thing that mattered to me was to be with my mom on her ninetieth birthday.

I needed to drop whatever I was doing and take a plane to Houston to see her. Nothing else was as important as that. Regardless that it was January, the beginning of the high season in Hawaii, the time of year when serious art collectors were in town and the best season for gallery owners like myself. To go anywhere, especially off-island in January, was not a good idea, but I had my priorities. That I didn't get the gallery's supplies and inventory fully stocked before leaving was unimportant. I left my paperwork, bills, press releases, and pending art exhibits in limbo and placed my trust in the universe and my husband to run the art gallery while I was gone.

A few months earlier, I'd been in Houston, helping my sister and brother-in-law move into their new apartment. I had stayed with my mom, spending quality time with her

then. But for some reason, I had the strong feeling to see
her again.

I'd be traveling on a tight budget, and I was okay with
that. This trip was going to be about hanging out with my
mom, not about shopping or gallery hopping or antiquing.

All I wanted to do was to be with her when she turned
ninety. I wanted to be the one who woke her up on her
birthday and sang "Las Mañanitas." She'd always done that
for me, on all my birthdays, and I wanted to do that for
her on her special day. I wanted to get her a birthday cake
and see her blow out the candles. And I wanted to see her
open presents. This time, my trip was going to be about
celebrating my mom's life, and I was more excited than I
had been in months.

Since my trip was pretty much last minute, there wasn't
much time to prepare or pack for the trip, so I grabbed
whatever stack of clean clothes I had sitting on the dryer
and jammed them in my carry-on. That was it. For once I
packed light. Besides the clothes on my back, I took a pair of
cargo pants, two T-shirts, sleep clothes, socks, one bra, and
a dozen panties. As far as I'm concerned, you can never have
too many panties.

The only thing I made sure I had room for in my cavern-
ous leather hobo bag was the digital photo frame I was giving
my mom for her birthday. I stuffed it neatly in between my
jacket and a shawl. I had spent days downloading pictures
that I thought she'd get a kick out of seeing. The photos were
of people, places, and things I often mentioned during our
daily phone calls. I downloaded pictures of my husband, our
three border collies, our best friends, the new house we're
building in an 'Ohi'a forest, our abundant flower gardens
with anthuriums and orchids of all colors and varieties, and
anything else I thought she'd find interesting. It would be a

way for her to actually see and, in some small way, participate in my life through the pictures.

My mom had a vivid imagination, and I knew she'd be able to transport herself to Hawaii every time she saw one of my prized cymbidium orchids or giant hāpuʻu ferns flash on the screen of the digital frame. I was sure it was the best present I'd ever given her, and I felt a sense of accomplishment, knowing it would be a total surprise.

The day of my flight passed quickly, and by early evening, I was heading out to Kona International Airport to catch my inter-island flight to Honolulu. I'd be taking the redeye flight on Continental directly to Houston. I had no idea at the time that Houston was in the middle of a cold snap. Living in Hawaii for nearly thirty years had left me relatively clueless as to how cold it can get during the winter months on the mainland, since the island temperatures are generally rather temperate.

However, I dislike being cold on an airplane so I wore my long-sleeved, taupe corduroy dress with jeans underneath. Just in case I got cold, I had the old black tweed collarless jacket and the shawl in my hobo bag. For a bit of flair, I wrapped my tan-and-white striped cotton jersey scarf around my neck. I've always had a thing for scarves.

As my husband and I were killing time before I boarded my flight to Honolulu, I saw a leggy little girl, maybe twelve years old, wearing a pair of Uggs. I remembered I had just gotten a pair of Uggs for Christmas, and they were in the back of my van. Something registered in my brain that taking my boots might be a good idea; they would certainly keep me warm on the plane ride. I remembered the time I had gone to Houston a few years earlier to celebrate Christmas with my mom and had shown up during a sudden harsh cold snap, wearing flip-flops and a short denim skirt and without a single piece of warm clothing. That was a mistake I never wanted to repeat. My husband ran back to the van to get the boots before my plane took off. After running clear across the airport parking lot, he got back with my Uggs just as my flight was starting to board. He stood there smiling, wiped the sweat off his face onto his T-shirt, and then gave me a tender hug and kiss goodbye. I crammed my boots into the tiny front zippered section of my carry-on. It made my suitcase look like it was nine months pregnant and on the verge of birthing baby carry-ons.

It was sweet of my husband to run all the way back out to our van just to get my boots . . . and those fuzzy boots kept me warm during my whole trip.

I arrived in Honolulu at 7:35 p.m. with ample time to wander the terminal, buy a good book to read, and get some dinner before my flight began boarding at 8:55 p.m. I decided to indulge for dinner so I headed straight to Pizza Hut, got my favorite cheese pizza and a bottle of water, and began to eat my dinner and relax before my flight. As I sat there in the food court, eating my pizza, I watched all the people coming and going and absent-mindedly flipped through my book. I felt a combination of exhaustion from the hectic day I'd had at the gallery and everything else leading up to my flight and elation, knowing what was waiting for me at the end of my flight.

Once I boarded the plane, found my seat, and put my carry-on in the overhead compartment, I knew the only things left for me to do were order a gin and tonic, put on my headset, watch the in-flight movie, and fall asleep halfway through the movie.

Next thing I became aware of was the sunlight sneaking in from some of the windows and the stewardess offering coffee and juice as a precursor to breakfast. It was approximately six thirty in the morning, mainland time, making that two thirty in the morning Hawaiian time. My stomach was in no mood for food so I ordered coffee with cream and water, lots of water to dilute the gin and tonic from the night before.

My heart began to pound with anticipation . . .

Though I had wanted to catch my mom off-guard and surprise her by landing on her doorstep unannounced, my sisters and I decided it was best to let her know in advance of my trip so she could prepare for my visit. Besides, she always loved to make a fuss when I visited, making sure she had vegetarian food that I like plus a new toothbrush, my own toothpaste, shampoo, conditioner, and of course, a box of chocolates. She always made sure that the guest towels were freshly laundered, as were the linens for the sofa bed I slept on. That was her way of welcoming me to her home.

Three hours later, we landed in Houston. I gathered up all my belongings, made my way through the sleepy crowd of fellow disembarking passengers, and began my trek to the baggage claim terminal that's on the street level and clear across the terminal. The Bush Intercontinental Airport in Houston, in my mind, is the size of a small city, and from the arrival gate to the baggage terminal is quite a journey. Some people ride in those six-seater carts, but I always walk all the way to the baggage claim area. Walking gave me a chance to call my mom and tell her I'd landed, call my sisters, and shake off any leftover drowsiness from my trip.

It was uncomfortably hot in the terminal due to the central heating, and by the time I'd made it down to baggage claim, I felt like I was suffocating and unable to breathe with all the heavy warm air. I broke out into a major sweat from the hike across the massive terminal.

As soon as I walked through the double glass sliding doors and was standing outside of the terminal, I was hit in the face with a blast of cold air that swept through the lower street level and I felt such a relief. I could breathe again. As I stood in the cold wind and my body temperature slowly began to drop, I felt the frigid air pass through all the layers of my clothes. I realized it actually felt like winter, a season that generally goes unnoticed in Hawaii where the weather rarely changes.

There I was in Houston, in the middle of January, in the middle of winter. Seems like my visits to Houston have always been during extremes of weather, either in the hottest part of the summer, the height of the hurricane season, or the coldest months of the year, never anything in between or moderate.

After waiting only a few minutes at the curb, I saw my sister Ana enter the terminal driving her new gold Saturn Outlook. She is always either early for her appointments or on time but never late. I crossed over to the special passenger pickup lanes where Ana had parked. She looked so cute when she got out of her car in a black leather skirt with a zebra-print cashmere sweater, a purple scarf tied around her neck, and purple suede boots. No coat, no jacket. She gave me a huge embrace with her tiny size 0 body. And just like that, I was all warm and toasty again.

Since we had time, being pretty close to my mom's, we took a detour so Ana could eat some lunch before dropping me off. We stopped at one of her favorite eateries in Town Square and ordered a cup of steaming hot tomato basil soup and sourdough bread. Even though after flights to the mainland my stomach often feels like it has a hangover since it's still on Hawaiian time and it doesn't know when it's time for a meal, I always manage to rise to the occasion and eat and drink whatever is put in front of me and do it with great gusto. Today was no exception.

After lunch, as we were heading back to our car, Ana was unable to resist the magnetic pull of the trendy boutique that was down the street from the restaurant where we'd just had lunch. We had no choice but to poke our heads in for a quick look. Then with all the self-restraint of seasoned renunciates, we went through the boutique quickly, merely scanning the displays of jewelry, clothes, purses, and shoes that had been artistically laid out in matching color schemes. It felt good to resist the temptation to shop on this trip.

The only thing we had left to do before going to my mom's was to stop at one of my favorite grocery stores, Fiesta, just a few blocks away from my mom's building. There were a few essentials I had to have, such as a birthday cake and candles. We chose our cake with careful and slow deliberation as we drooled over the overwhelming choices. We finally opted for one large dark-chocolate cake with dark-chocolate icing, decorated with pink roses, plus four small individual pieces of cake, all different varieties as backup cakes. Once that important task was completed, we picked out other necessities such as pan dulce, fresh ranchero cheese (the moist, crumbly, and salty white variety), a big stack of freshly made flour tortillas, a handful of Mexican limes, and a six-pack of Corona beer. My mom had already stockpiled the vegetarian beans because she knew I love my beans. I've had a love affair with beans ever since I was a child and able to eat solid foods.

We finally arrived at my mom's at around twelve thirty. I can't adequately describe how sweet and happy my mom looked when she saw me walk through the door. She was this petite and frail wisp of a woman with a big smile, large bright-brown eyes, short silver hair with soft bangs, and perfectly shaped black eyebrows. She had never plucked, shaped, waxed, or dyed her eyebrows her whole life, and they were still totally black and flawlessly arched, making a striking frame for those gentle and soulful eyes.

She'd suffered the last few years with osteoporosis, so she didn't like to go out much due to the discomfort she felt in her body. In her prime, she was gorgeous, and even at ninety, she was still beautiful, having aged with grace and dignity.

This was the thirteenth of January, the day before her birthday. I had thought we'd try to get my two sisters and their families together for a simple meal and birthday cake. But my mom wanted absolutely no extra fanfare. She didn't want anyone to make a big deal out of her birthday and insisted she'd much rather it be kept simple. What she really wanted to do was eat shrimp at a Red Lobster restaurant. So my sisters and I made plans to take my mom to Red Lobster for lunch on her birthday, the following day.

The next morning, I woke up early, snuck into my mom's bedroom, and broke out in a round of "Las Mañanitas." She was still in bed, under her warm flannel covers, enjoying that sleepy moment when all you want to do is maintain the perfect balance of your warm sheets and the arrangement of your pillow under your neck. She was surprised and I was happy. After we reminisced about some of the birthdays I'd had when I was a child, she got up and said it was time for coffee.

I went to the kitchen and turned on the coffeepot that was already set to brew. My mom entered the living room, still in her pajamas, pushing her walker. She giggled as I started up with the "Mañanitas" song again, and she kept walking in the direction of her kitchen. Always the mom, she asked me what she could make me for breakfast. On that note, I placed my hands on her narrow boney shoulders, turned her gently around, and invited her to sit down in her recliner, relax, and watch her favorite morning news programs while I brought her a cup of coffee.

Being there for my mom's birthday may have made her happy, but actually being able to greet her first thing in the morning, sing "Las Mañanitas," make her breakfast, and fuss over her a little left me feeling even happier.

My mom turned on the local news station to check on the weather as I got our breakfast together. I decided I would make my mom one of her personal favorites for breakfast, *chilaquiles*. Of course that means you also need beans that have been refried with onions, flour tortillas with butter, papaya slices, and Mexican pastry that I'd bought the day before.

As I was in the kitchen, sautéing the thinly sliced onion, I turned my attention to the stack of corn tortillas I'd placed on the cutting board. When I make chilaquiles, I like to slice the tortillas into chunky pieces, one inch square. You can also just tear them unceremoniously, but I like how the tortillas feel when they are stacked in threes or fours and you cut through them all at once. You feel the texture of the tortillas as the knife cuts through all the layers and hear the sound as the knife slices through the tortillas on the wooden cutting board. As strange as that might sound, that's part of the experience for me; all my senses are tuned in to the preparation, one step at a time. As soon as the onions are done sweating and beginning to gather a golden color, I add the tortillas plus a little extra olive oil and a pinch of salt. I keep an eye on them so the tortillas and onions don't burn.

I poured my mom a warm-up and brought out a slice of papaya with a slice of lime to get her breakfast started.

My mom then lowered the volume on the television and said, "*No vamos a poder salir hoy porque está muy frío afuera con lluvia y no quiero pescar un resfrío. No, mejor cancelamos todo. No necesito comer camarones. A la mejor me enfermo si como camarones.*"

According to the weather report on the local news station, the temperatures were going to hover in the mid- and upper-thirties all day with a chance of continued light drizzle and possibly sleet. As a result, my mom had just decided to cancel all our plans for her birthday celebration due to the cold weather. She didn't want to go outside in such bad weather. I couldn't blame her.

But part of me was disappointed by this turn of events. I wanted to do something special for my mom on her birthday. But that wasn't going to happen. She assured me that if the weather cleared up by the weekend, we could go out then for her birthday shrimp.

Well, that settled our agenda for the day, and I went back to the kitchen to pick up where I had left off . . . the chilaquiles. Normally I make my chilaquiles pretty spicy, but my mom can't handle the heavy spices anymore, so I go easy on the peppers.

"Do you want red or green salsa on the chilaquiles?" I asked.

My mom didn't waste a second and responded, "*Salsa verde, con quesito blanco también.*" (Green salsa with white cheese too.) That sounded good to me, and I added tomatillos, onion, garlic, salt, and Serrano chiles with a little farmer's cheese crumbled on top. I got the salsa ready to go and the beans were already being refried with a little bit of chopped onions in olive oil. As soon as my tortillas were golden yet not too crunchy, I added the salsa, and whoosh, all the smells, sounds, and steam rose up as I added the wet ingredient to the tortillas.

I got out the Falfurrias butter and set the kitchen table. My mom made her way to the table and sat down. Plating her dish with a generous portion of chilaquiles and beans, I then handed it to her. I couldn't resist heating up a few fresh flour tortillas. They are totally unnecessary, but I love how the flavors work together. The combination of flour tortillas and chilaquiles reminds me of the flavor of tamales. I used my flour tortilla to scoop up my food. My dad would constantly frown at my tortilla etiquette, saying it was unrefined to eat that way. He insisted we eat with a fork, roll up our tortilla, and take a bite of that with each forkful of food. I still use my tortillas to scoop up my food.

My mom loved her breakfast. She ate everything I put on her plate, which was rare because she normally ate tiny portions of food. She said her appetite was always better when I visited her. I gave her another coffee warm-up and brought out some of the Mexican pastries. She took half a *marranito* (a gingerbread cookie shaped like a pig), and I took the other half. As we dunked our marranitos in our coffee, the phone rang, the first of many calls my mom would have that day.

It was my sister Nene calling from her classroom. She put her phone on speaker, and all the children in her class began singing "Las Mañanitas" to my mom. It was like having a surprise birthday party in a way. My mom never expected to hear a choir of fourth graders singing "Las Mañanitas." Her bright brown eyes began to glaze over with tears, and slowly, the tears trickled down her face. Something told me this was going to be a great day for my mom, with or without the shrimp.

The phone began to ring nonstop. Her girlfriends and my siblings began calling, one by one. There was one brief break in between all the calls where she actually had time to get out of her pajamas and get dressed, do her hair, and put on a little face powder and lipstick. She put on her rings and a favorite ivory seagull necklace that I had bought her over forty years ago. She looked elegant as always.

As soon as she sat back down in her recliner, the calls started coming in again . . . my cousin calling from Nuevo Laredo, our old neighbor from Brownsville, more friends, all the grandchildren, one by one . . . this was an all-day event.

While my mom was busy enjoying her moment, I went in the kitchen to clean up and put things away. Then I took a shower. When I came out of the shower, she was still talking to someone on the phone. Amazing how many people had their thoughts on my mom on her birthday. I realized that she had quite the fan club of friends and well-wishers, and that made me feel good about her independence. She loved her life just like it was. She was living in her own apartment, and she liked that independence and freedom. At ninety, I think that's a brave way to face your days and nights.

I looked out the living room window to check on the weather, and it looked like the rain had stopped, so I asked my mom if she'd like to go for an early dinner. "Mami, we want to celebrate your birthday by taking you to Red Lobster for shrimp, just like you wanted. It's not raining now. Want to go?"

"*No, mi hijita, no se va poder hacer hoy. Hace mucho frío y no me quiero resfriar. Sera otro día, si Dios quiere*," she said. (No, my little daughter, it will not be possible to do it today. It is very cold, and I don't want to catch a cold. There will be another day, God willing.)

She'd made up her mind. Her birthday outing wasn't going to happen today. So I finally dropped it. I realized that it wasn't about taking her out to do something special on her birthday, like eating shrimp at Red Lobster. We were already doing something special for her birthday, maybe even more special than going out to a restaurant. We were just hanging out together, and that was priceless.

It seemed like the perfect time to give her the present I'd brought from home. I grabbed it out of my hobo bag and handed it to her. She tore through the wrapping paper and opened the box and said, "*Un marco. Gracias mijita, que bonito.*" (A picture frame. Thank you. How pretty.)

The tone in her voice sounded disappointed, but not for long. I took the frame out of her hands, plugged the cords into the frame and the wall outlet, and turned on her frame. Once all the images came on the screen, she couldn't believe it. She'd never seen a digital frame before, and it was definitely the biggest surprise of the day.

Just as I had imagined, she was transported to Hawaii, and I began to share my life with her. She began pointing out, "Oh, that must be your best friends, Margaret and Michael." . . . "There are my grandchildren" (meaning my dogs, of course). . . . "Look at the gardens . . . how beautiful." . . . "The sunset . . . the orchids." . . . This went on for forty-five minutes. Then the photos began to repeat themselves, and she watched everything all over again. In fact, the frame stayed on the whole time I was there. She never tired of looking at the pictures.

My sister Ana dropped in on her way home from work. She told my mom that she'd made the right decision to stay indoors. The weather was extremely cold, and due to the rain, the roads were icy. Ana reassured my mom (and me too) that we'd have plenty of time to take her out for a birthday treat.

So we did the only thing we could do—bring out the birthday cake! We put candles on all four smaller pieces of cake, saving her big cake for another day, and sang "Happy Birthday."

It was fun and my mom loved it. She picked out the chocolate cake, which was no big surprise to us since we knew it was her favorite. Mami was happy, and that was what was important.

Nene showed up just as we were about to begin eating cake. Her timing was perfect. She wanted to spend the weekend with us and make it a long birthday weekend celebration. We had an all-girls weekend extravaganza, and I couldn't have asked for more.

All my hopes for being there to celebrate my mom's life came to fruition. I was able to sing to her "Las Mañanitas" first thing in the morning, make her breakfast, see her open her present, give her a birthday cake, and watch her blow out the candles. Even more than that, I was able to spend the rest of the week with her talking about her life and, more importantly, listening.

That birthday weekend, Nene and I heard many of my mom's childhood stories that were filled with memories as sharp and detailed as if they had just happened the day before. There were some stories that I'd already heard, but this time it felt like they were also becoming part of my own life, of my own history, and maybe even part of my own future.

Nene and I both knew how lucky we were to have had that special time with Mami. Some stories we heard that weekend were told to us for the first time . . . it was a lot to absorb, to try to store in our own memories. But it wasn't all serious talk; it never is when you get us girls together. We made sure there were plenty of cold Coronas to last us through the long weekend.

To say we laughed a lot would be an understatement. We basically couldn't stop laughing all weekend. My mom had the same silly sense of humor that her sister had, both natural-born comedians. And Nene inherited that wonderful trait. Hanging out at my mom's apartment doesn't sound overly exciting, but it was, trust me. My mom, Nene, and I all laughed like girlfriends, and that was special. We drank Coronas like they were on sale, ate all day long, talked incessantly, and joked around as much as possible.

BUELI, RECENTLY WIDOWED, WITH TÍA LOLIS ON THE LEFT AND MY MOM (ABOUT TWO YEARS OLD) SITTING ON A FOUNTAIN AT A RELATIVE'S HOME, QUERÉTARO, MEXICO, 1922.

On the flip side, my sister and I were saddened by some of the stories we heard about my mom's childhood. She went through some painful experiences of separation, from losing her father when she was a baby to being separated from her own mother later in life. I had no idea how incredibly awesome my mom was. Yes, I've always thought she was the perfect mom. But as an individual human being, apart from being my mom, in my realizing what she went through in her life and seeing how amazing she turned out, well, it proves she was made of gold.

Sunday morning arrived quickly, and my mom announced that it was the perfect day to go out and enjoy the sun and some birthday shrimp.

And we did just that. We all got dressed and then bundled up my mom with a wool jacket, scarf, and knit cap to keep out the cold. Ana picked us up, and we headed out to Red Lobster for the birthday meal my mom had asked for.

There was no need to rush the day, so we took our time eating. We finished off lunch with a special chocolate cake that the waitress brought out with birthday candles, and everyone in the restaurant joined us in singing her "Happy Birthday" and cheering her on for her ninetieth.

I knew Mami would be embarrassed by all the attention and fanfare. And she was. But what the heck, it was her ninetieth, and there was no way in the world we were going to let it pass without a little bit of embarrassment.

One more thing we did to celebrate her birthday and make it a perfect day was to take Mami shopping. How could all of us girls be together and not get in a little shopping time? The temperature was a mellow sixty-two and sunny. My mom felt full of energy and actually wanted to walk around the shopping plaza. We went to the store my sister and I had seen on the day I arrived.

My mom tootled around the boutique, pushing her walker, looking at all the jewelry, purses, scarves, and hats. It melted my heart seeing her being one of the girls.

After all, my visit was about celebrating my mom's life, about honoring her long and incredible journey. Truth be told, my mom's ninetieth birthday served as a reminder to me . . . about making time in my hectic life for my own family who lives so far away. This visit showed me the importance of spending quality time with my mom while she was still healthy enough to enjoy my visits and sassy enough to scold me and tease me.

I hung out with my mom as if we both had all the time in the world to relax and linger in that moment of perfect, sublime togetherness.

In the City of Gods

M Y PARENTS DID EVERYTHING GOOD PARENTS ALWAYS
DO . . . spend the best part of their young adult lives
feeding, clothing, nurturing, protecting, loving, and edu-
cating their children. It's totally possible, if not probable,
my parents had no idea to what degree their lives would
impact my own. And it's possible that I was also unaware
of the scope of their influence until much later in my life.
There were far-reaching actions that altered the course of
my life. Of course that was something I didn't understand
in my youth. How could I?

And on a few occasions, they played an even greater role
in my life, that of being the sole person who was at the right
place, at the right time . . . to save my life.

It was the summer of '68. My mom, Nene, and I were
spending our vacation with my dad in Mexico City. His job
at the time required that he make a permanent move. I hated
that our family was separated. I wanted nothing more than
for us to be together. But he wanted my sister and me to
finish our education in Texas and to go on to college. Visit

my dad in Mexico City, absolutely, but to relocate us permanently, absolutely not! Nene and I had already laid out a torrent of arguments and tears regarding our wishes, but once my dad's mind was made up, it was unlikely he'd ever change it. And he never did. I'm sure my mom also tried on many occasions to change his mind, but he wouldn't budge. He'd made many sacrifices to give us a better life and felt he knew what was best for us.

I look back on those days and realize my dad did know what was best . . . we were able to get a college education and do whatever it was we wanted to do with our lives, to go in any direction and pursue any dream we wanted to.

Even though I had no say in where I lived during those years and going back to Brownsville at the end of summer vacation was always filled with so much sadness, while I was in Mexico City, I loved every minute of it. I don't remember a time when I was more connected to loving my life. Was it the budding hormones of a sixteen-year-old that kept me in the moment? Who can say?

My dad made sure we always had some activity or adventure to keep us busy, entertained, and out of trouble. Either he would plan activities for us to do with my mom while he was working, or we'd make our own plans. One year he hired a chauffeur/travel guide to take us around to many of the big cultural sites because he simply didn't have the time.

On the weekends, my dad took advantage of being off to do special things with us. We would take day trips to visit cities with rich historical backgrounds such as Puebla. It was famous for its hand-painted Talavera tile and for its internationally acclaimed cuisine, including the well-known dish, *mole poblano*. Most meaningful to me, however, was that it was the birthplace of my maternal grandmother. We had family roots in Puebla. The city is located to the east of

Mexico City. We'd leave early in the morning and make it by late morning. We'd walk around the *zócalo* (town square), take our time strolling through the historic downtown area, which was known as the "cradle of Mexican Baroque," take photographs, do a little shopping, visit churches, have a late lunch, and then head back home.

The following weekend, Papi would pick another town he wanted to show us like Cuernavaca, south of Mexico City. And then the following week, we might do Taxco, the silver capital of Mexico, which was southeast of Mexico City. Of special interest to me was that the full name of the city was actually Taxco de Alarcón, and Alarcón was our surname. Taxco was always one of my favorite cities with so many cathedrals and silver shops to explore.

Sometimes we'd go to the local museums in Mexico City such as the National Museum of Anthropology, spending a few hours looking at all the special exhibits, and then my dad would take us to a wonderful restaurant for lunch or dinner. It was always a big adventure and one that made us feel cultured.

Of all those trips, there is one that stands out in my mind that we did on a cool and cloudy Saturday morning.

My dad decided it would be the perfect day to drive out of town and head northeast in search of the ruins of Teotihuacán. It was a thirty-mile drive from the city, making it a pleasant day trip. He told us we were going to see some ancient pyramids and ruins.

My older sister Ana was visiting us from Houston for a few weeks. So Ana, Nene, and I got in the back seat of the car while my mom rode up front with my dad. We left our apartment by nine in the morning, giving us plenty of time to see the ruins. Papi told us we'd most likely stop at a restaurant on our way back home for a late lunch or early dinner.

To understand what our road trips were generally like, you need to know a couple of things about my dad. He was never a chatty kind of person. Not big on small talk. I never heard him have a trivial conversation with anyone, ever. He was a serious person. Generally, a car ride with my dad could be quiet, if not altogether dull. He would make occasional comments or point out something of interest or historical importance, such as a building or monument or big fountain. He just never rambled.

Also, he had strict rules about traveling in a car—no games, toys, food, books, drinks; nothing extra in the car. A car was for transportation purposes only. So as a kid it was rather boring to take a long car ride with him. We'd eventually have lots of fun once we arrived at our destination. But the drive itself was never exciting.

Once he almost broke that rule about no food in the car. During the summer of 1970, the year I graduated from high school, my parents and I were on our way to Acapulco for a few days' vacation when my dad saw a child by the road side selling *nopalitos*, peeled edible cactus, and he pulled over to buy a bag. He was so fastidious and at times could be finicky about what he ate that my mom and I were both shocked to see him stop to buy food from a roadside urchin. Anyway, he pulled over quickly, hopped out of the car, and paid the little boy twice what he was asking so he'd have a little extra money as a tip. My mom and I got out of the car and walked over to my dad as he was neatly opening the plastic bag of nopalitos. My parents immediately dove into those delicacies and said they were delicious and tender. I've never been a lover of nopalitos or okra for that matter. Both have one thing in common, a slimy characteristic that I can't tolerate. I suppose the fact that my parents stood outside of the car to eat the cactus meant no rules had been breached.

Another interesting fact about my dad was his intelligence; you might even say he was brilliant. He was also ambidextrous. His neat and stylized signature was exactly the same each time he wrote it, whether he used his left or right hand. One time I asked him to sign his signature on two pieces of onionskin stationary, first using his right hand and then his left. When I placed them on top of each other, they were identical. I was amazed and the look on his face said, "You doubted my talent, silly girl?"

My dad was the sort of person who read the *Encyclopedia Britannica* for fun every evening, and he eventually, over the course of several years, had read through every volume. He knew a whole lot about many different things.

During the drive out to the pyramids, my dad decided to pass on some information he'd read regarding the Aztec civilization and the pyramids. That he even decided to have a lengthy conversation while driving in a car was a bit of a surprise. Cars, after all, were for traveling in and not for idle talk.

He mentioned that the Aztecs had named the area Teotihuacán, which means "The City of Gods." The Aztecs arrived after the pyramids had already been built, so it was some other indigenous culture that had built them long before the Aztecs discovered them. They are considered by many to be among the most important in the world and the Pyramid of the Sun happens to be the third largest in the world. I was fascinated. At one time during my early college years, I considered becoming an archeologist. For all I know, the seed of curiosity might have been planted way back then, on the day I climbed the pyramids.

Teotihuacán, with the Pyramid of the Sun, Pyramid of the Moon, Temple of Quetzalcóatl, Avenue of the Dead, Citadel, and other temples and ceremonial structures, were built in alignment to stars and planets. It was a hub of sorts for cosmic energy. And there had been ancient ceremonial rituals, some of which included human sacrifice. This was both fascinating and a bit scary to me.

Once my dad was finished with his talk, it suddenly got quiet again.

We kept driving along the highway that would eventually take us to Teotihuacán. The car windows were all rolled down with a fresh breeze blowing through. My dad rolled up the sleeves of his white shirt while my mom covered her hair with a lightweight, floral-print scarf and tied it under her chin to keep her hair from blowing around and getting messy. The three of us girls in the back seat really didn't care how our hair looked. The air felt so refreshing; we let the wind do whatever it wanted.

As the three of us were being lulled into a narcotic-like trance with the wind whipping and swirling around in the car, the monotonous sound of the car tires on the open road, and the silence that had now engulfed the air space, there came a sudden and chilling change of energy.

Out of the corner of my eye, I saw my dad looking again and again into his rearview mirror with a dramatic change in his facial expressions, one I'd never seen before, and it didn't look good, though I didn't know exactly what it meant.

Suddenly, he stepped on the gas pedal. We were immediately jolted out of our stupor by the whiplash we felt from the abrupt jump in speed of our small sedan, now propelling us at seventy-five miles an hour . . . in the wrong lane. I was in shock . . . I didn't know what was going on until seconds later it became clear.

As my dad veered into the southbound lane, another car was speeding up to us in the right lane, dangerously close to our car. As I looked over to my right, the car had come up right next to us at the same high speed. There were two men in the front seat. Both of them had dark-colored ski caps pulled over their faces with only their eyes exposed. They were trying to force my dad off the highway and onto the shoulder of the road.

I'd heard stories about people being robbed on the open highway in Mexico. And up to that point, I thought they were just unfounded rumors. Apparently not. As I learned later, this was a common technique bandits used to scare people off the road in order to rob them.

My dad, while driving like a maniac, reached over my mom's lap, managed to open the glove compartment on the passenger's side, and started to dig through the contents. The next thing I saw was even more surreal than the *bandidos* trying to force us off the road—my dad pulling out a small silver-barreled handgun with a black handle. He began waving it around so the men could see he had a gun.

My mom looked like she was getting ready to pass out or throw up or perhaps both. In spite of the ashen tone of her face, adrenaline must have kicked in, and within a few seconds that felt like minutes, she appeared to have regained control of her emotions.

Meanwhile, my dad shouted all kinds of obscenities and threats out the window at the men, all the while waving his gun around. I'd never heard so many swear words before, especially not in Spanish. When he'd finished trying to scare the bandidos away, he set the shiny silver handgun in the corner of the dashboard so it was unmistakably visible through the window.

My method of dealing with what was going on was to shut out the violence to a certain degree. It felt like I was in some kind of bubble where the shouting was muted and sounded far off and removed, like this was happening in a bad dream and not in reality.

But it was happening and I wasn't dreaming.

Once the men saw that my dad was armed, they slammed on their brakes and slowed way down, made a U-turn, and headed back in the other direction to whatever dark, crusty, and smelly hole they'd crawled out of.

My dad then lowered his speed and safely got us back into the correct lane. He took the gun off the dashboard and placed it right back into the glove compartment. Papi never said a word about what had just happened. No comment. Just kept on driving in silence.

We sat there, looking at each other, stunned and thinking, "What just happened?" I didn't even know my dad owned a gun. If someone had asked me the day before if my dad owned a gun, I would have laughed and said, "No way! Not only does he not own a gun, he's probably never even seen a real gun and wouldn't know how to use it if you put one in his hand!" Well, how about that? My dad in fact did own a gun, and I began to believe he knew exactly what to do with one too. You know, that was a real eye-opener for me. It was also the first time I'd ever seen a gun.

The rest of our drive out to the pyramids was rather uneventful, a development which we were ecstatic about. Suddenly there was something to be said for boring, after all.

We finally arrived, all in one piece. My dad drove around the parking lot and found a spot close to the entrance. Once we'd nudged each other out of the car, gotten a dose of that crisp, pure mountain air, the kind that seems to clean out your lungs with the first deep inhalation, and had given our legs a good stretch, our eyes were able to settle in on the landscape that surrounded us. It hardly looked believable.

The area was strewn with ruins—stairs carved from stone, tumbled stone walls, remnants of stone structures in various stages of decay and reconstruction, stone carvings of deities, long passages and walkways, ancient frescos on the crumbling walls, huge pyramids, all kinds of archaeological remains I'd never seen before.

We walked around for a long time, trying to absorb its historical significance. There was a vibration in the air that felt electric and palpable. It was the energy emanating from the pyramids. I mean if the towering Pyramid of the Sun wasn't enough to impress you, there were the Pyramid of the Moon, the Temple of Quetzalcóatl, the Avenue of the Dead that is miles long and mind-boggling, and the crumbled remains of wall murals in which you still see jaguar paintings. Intricate stone carvings of their gods such as the feathered serpent Quetzalcóatl and the rain god Tláloc were visible.

My dad suggested we climb the Pyramid of the Sun before it got too late. My mom didn't want to go up to the top of the pyramid, so she chose to stay behind with Ana. So just my dad, Nene, and I climbed up those 248 steps to the top. My dad appeared to have no trouble climbing all those steps, an amazing feat considering he was a heavy smoker and went through at least a pack of unfiltered Lucky Strikes a day. He actually beat us to the top.

For Nene and me, it was slow going. The steps were rather narrow, not at all like a modern stairway. The steps looked like they had been built for tiny feet. Someone told me that the steps were built that way because people climbed them sideways, which made perfect sense in light of the size of the steps, but I wasn't sure if that was true. We inched our way up, bit by bit. As I ascended the stone steps of the pyramid, I realized that Aztecs had done the same thing long ago; some of them may have reached the top of the pyramid only to become human sacrifices.

Once we got to the top, I couldn't believe what I saw and felt. I was standing in an ancient spot, gazing upon the same panorama the Aztecs had seen. We walked all over the top of the pyramid, looking down at the people below us on the ground. They suddenly looked like insignificant ants milling about aimlessly. My mom and sister looked like barely visible specks on the landscape.

From where we were standing, we could see the Pyramid of the Moon and look down to the Avenue of the Dead and on to the other ruins of temples and ceremonial buildings and mounds of tumbled stones.

I also noticed how quiet it was up there. You might even say it was an absence of sound. Occasionally, you could hear the wind passing and a few people talking quietly in the distance, but mostly people were just looking. There was an expression of reverence mixed with awe painted on the faces of many of the people at the top of the Sun Pyramid.

As I walked over to one side, I looked out as far as I could see. And what I saw was more than my young mind could assimilate. At the time, I had no words in my vocabulary to adequately describe what I had experienced. But I know that it gave me chills.

As I turned around, Nene chimed, "Smile." And she took a picture of me standing there by the edge. The second after she snapped the photo, a strong gust of wind came up; it felt as though it took hold of my whole body, and I began to lose my balance. I was a split second away from falling down the side of the pyramid and becoming a sixteen-year-old virgin sacrifice.

The strong hands of my father came out of nowhere, grabbed on to the front of my red bandana print dress, and hung onto me for my dear life. He pulled me back from the edge and stood me straight up. He just stood there looking at me, like he couldn't believe what had just happened. I quickly moved away from the edge and hung onto my dad and gave him the biggest hug I think I'd ever given him or any other person in my life. I started to cry from the shock when I realized how close I'd come to becoming one more sacrifice.

What was so strange was that I didn't even remember seeing my dad standing near my sister as she was taking my photo; he just seemed to appear out of nowhere.

When we got back down to the bottom of the pyramid, we found my mom and sister just where we'd left them and told them the whole story. Of course everyone was relieved that I hadn't fallen, especially my mom, but the story sounded almost too dramatic to believe.

On the drive back home, my dad told us that it was common practice to bury the skeletons of the children they had sacrificed in the steps of the pyramids and they had discovered that some of the temples had large caves or pits underneath them that also contained human remains.

Great . . . the sun god, after all those eons, was still hungry for more sacrifices. Hard to imagine.

Forty-two years later, after countless moves from one house to another, from one state to another, and several times back and forth across the Pacific, I was still able to hang onto something pretty special—the picture my sister took of me that day on the top of the pyramid.

I was wearing a great big smile on my face, oblivious to what was just about to happen.

The experience at the pyramids left me feeling sober. The following morning, I felt subdued and quiet all day. I had no desire to be out spending my time in frivolous abandon. Not that I was having some incredible existential breakthrough. I just wanted to stay home, stay put, and stay on the ground.

As I look back to that day in particular, I begin to understand the depth of a parent/child relationship. It can go way beyond the realm of the physical and at times can cross over to the psychic.

Sometimes parents are there to extend our time on earth. They listen to their intuition and appear to be at the right place at the right time. By grabbing onto my dress that day at the pyramid, my dad extended the story of my life. He gave me a chance to add many more chapters.

And as I sit here writing this story, I'm reminded of other times he was destined to be there for me. Maybe it was a special connection we shared, or maybe it was my dad listening to his intuition. Whatever it was, there will always be a certain amount of mystery to our connection, and there will always be love.

Chocolate Milk

I WAS ONLY SIX YEARS OLD AND A REAL CUTIE-PIE. I'd recently gotten my waist-length, golden-brown locks cut. My mom knew she wouldn't be able to keep up with my hair once I started first grade. She had four other children to worry about. So my long, wavy, sun-kissed hair was a casualty of the first grade.

My mom had taken me to a beauty shop in Matamoros that all her friends went to, and I remember the gut-wrenching feeling I had as I looked in the mirror. I didn't recognize myself. I broke down in tears. I didn't have that little-girl look anymore. Instead, I looked a bit like a street urchin right out of Spanky and Our Gang.

The hairdresser braided my hair first, then chopped off my braids, and handed them to my mom like some kind of trophy or souvenir, reminiscent of a matador being handed the ear of the bull he has just defeated in the bullring. The lady gave me a classic Buster-Brown bowl haircut, no kidding. Straight bangs right across my forehead and the rest, short, practically up to my ears. Thank goodness my mom had the sense to have the butchery done a couple of weeks before school started.

The interesting thing was, there were numerous casualties in the first grade, which began to chip away at how I viewed the world.

Of course the very first "first grade hurdle" was getting over the loss of my hair. After the shock of having my precious locks chopped off, I learned at a very young age that it was, after all, only hair and that hair generally grew right back. There would be plenty more where that came from. In fact I felt sure there was no limit to how much hair I'd be able to grow out in my lifetime.

My mom told me that my haircut wasn't the end of the world and to save my tears for when she died. If I kept crying, she warned me, I'd run out of tears and wouldn't have any left for her funeral. Hmm . . . I wondered for the longest time if that was really true. It wasn't until after I'd cried about one thing or another on countless occasions that I realized my tears, like my hair, always had an endless supply.

Even as I got older, if I cried about anything for too long, my mom would always say the same thing, "It's not the end of the world so stop crying. You'll run out of tears and won't be able to cry at my funeral." Once I realized there was no way I was ever going to run out of tears, I felt relieved to know that there would most likely be a deep and aching well of tears from which to do her justice at her funeral.

Another thing I became aware of in the first grade was that I was different from my classmates. Most of the other kids in my class were Anglo, and I was Mexican American. I mean, at the beginning of the school year, I was unaware that I was Mexican American; I was just like all the other kids as far as I was concerned. I didn't know there was any difference between people . . . those labels were unfamiliar to me.

MY FIRST GRADE MUG SHOT.
MISSING ARE ALL MY LONG GOLDEN CURLS.

In my family, we embraced our culture, for sure, but it was never pointed out that I had a Mexican heritage. It was just what it was, my heritage. I figured everyone had one, maybe like mine or maybe not, but had one, nonetheless. It never occurred to me that people would be labeled by their heritage.

In my class there was this nice boy that the other kids picked on. His name was Brady. We sat next to each other since both our last names started with an A and we were seated alphabetically. That proved to be a curse for me throughout my school years since I always got stuck sitting up front by the teacher. Anyway, Brady was a little heavier set than the other boys, though not by much, so they teased him, calling him chubby. I didn't like that they picked on him. There was more than one occasion when I stood up for him, and I was sure he'd have done the same for me.

Maybe it was his love of food that made him an easy target. He was in charge of going to the cafeteria every day to pick up our little cartons of milk we got for our break. He had also taken responsibility for handing out the milk. He always picked out the carton he thought was the heaviest. Before handing you your milk, he'd hold it up in his right hand and another carton in his left and go back and forth trying to decide if one was heavier than the other. Anytime he thought a carton was a tiny bit heavier, he'd put it aside. By the time he'd gone around the room he had a few choice cartons set aside. I bet that was the real reason he got picked on.

For the snack, I always ordered regular milk, and Brady always ordered chocolate milk. One day, after he'd passed around the milk, I'd gotten my carton of milk, and he had his, we sat down at our desks to take our break. Just as I started to open my little carton of milk, he stopped me short of drinking it.

He said, "Hey, wait a minute. We should switch our milk." And he grabbed my milk carton and gave me his chocolate milk.

I was stunned and said, "Why did you do that? Why should we switch?"

Brady looked at me with a straightforward look on his face and said, "Well, because you're brown like chocolate milk and I'm white like regular white milk. You should drink your own color, that's why."

I just sat there wondering what he meant by that. How was I brown like chocolate milk? And how was he like white milk? I couldn't figure it out. I didn't know why he said that, but somehow it made me feel different and not in a good way. Like there was something wrong with being chocolate milk. What did he mean by "drink your own color"?

The fact was I was pretty color-blind. My parents never pointed out skin color differences, so how would I have ever known there was a difference?

I grabbed back my white milk carton from him, gave him his brown milk carton back, and said, "Brady, I don't like chocolate milk, so there!" I got up, found an empty desk on the other side of the room, closer to the teacher's desk, and sat down. As I drank my milk, I felt sick to my stomach. I didn't know why I felt sick, but I did. My friend, whom I had often stuck up for, had just said something that felt hurtful, and I didn't even know what he meant by his innuendo. He may have had no idea what he meant or maybe he did, but either way, it felt like I'd been stung by a wasp.

I didn't say anything to my mom when I got home from school that day. What I did tell my mom was that I didn't want to get milk at school anymore so she didn't need to give me milk money. She said, "*¿Y porqué? ¿Siempre te gustaba y ahora de repente ya no quieres tomar leche?*" (Why? You have always liked it, and now all of a sudden, you don't want to get milk?) The thing about my mom was that she was intuitive, and no matter what you were trying to hide from her, she knew there was a whole lot of the story she wasn't hearing. Sometimes she'd push you until you cracked, and other times she'd just let it ride until you were ready to spill the beans on your own. So she grilled me. I nodded my head yes, I didn't want to get milk, and kept my mouth shut. The following days, when everyone else got their milk,

I went out the front door of the classroom and drank water from the water fountain, even though the water came out lukewarm and had a strange metallic taste.

My week went by with me feeling not especially friendly towards Brady anymore, and I think he felt a little awkward too. By Friday of that week, I got hit again.

We were in the cafeteria. Brady was sitting across from me, and there were a couple of girls from my class on either side of me. They took out their lunches. Annie had a baloney sandwich with Miracle Whip on white bread and a dill pickle on the side, and Vicky had a tuna fish sandwich on white bread with a handful of potato chips. Brady had two sandwiches, one was a meatloaf sandwich with catsup on white bread, and the second was peanut butter and grape jelly on white bread. Nothing I hadn't seen before in the lunchroom.

That wasn't the type of food I liked to eat for lunch. Since I lived close to home, my sister and I usually walked home for lunch. My favorite lunch was a bowl of beans and corn or flour tortillas, whatever was handy. My sister and I took our lunches to school that day since my mom wasn't going to be home at lunchtime; she was going to the Greyhound bus station in town to pick up my granny who was coming for a visit. So that day, my mom packed us both a great lunch.

I put my lunch pail on top of the table and took out a cloth napkin my mom had packed. I set it on the table. Then I took out my little lunch bundle that was neatly wrapped in wax paper with all the ends tucked in so it had a tight seal, and I began to unroll it ceremoniously onto the napkin.

It was one of my all-time favorites, a flour tortilla with refried beans, rice, *chorizo con lluevo* (scrambled egg with chorizo sausage), and a little sprinkle of white Mexican ranchero cheese. Today you would call my lunch a *burrito*, but

back then, no one called it a burrito. Mexican food had yet
to gain global mainstream status, nor had the burrito gained
such worldwide fame that it has now garnered. Things were
so different back then . . .

There I was, completely focused on the flavorful burrito
I was getting ready to sink my teeth into, completely oblivious to my friends sitting around me. In fact, I had no reason to think anyone was even looking at what I was doing.
Once my divine burrito had been unfurled from its wrapping, I picked it up with both hands, and as it approached
my mouth, I could smell the rich and spicy aroma of the
chorizo, smelling strongly of *comino* (cumin), mixed with
the pungent Mexican cheese. Oh man, did that smell like
heaven or what?

I proceeded to take my first mouth-watering bite. Just
then, as I did that, I looked up and saw Brady pointing his
finger at me, laughing. I chewed my first bite, swallowed
quickly, and went for the second bite. I then looked to
my left at Annie and to my right at Vicky, and they were
also laughing. I couldn't believe it. Why were they laughing? What was so funny about my lunch? Hadn't they ever
seen a burrito before? Brady, Annie, and Vicky were laughing with their mouths wide open and full of food. In fact,
as Brady laughed, half of the food in his mouth fell out
all over the cafeteria table, and it looked like some of his
meatloaf had gotten smeared all over the front of his light-
green T-shirt.

I looked down at my cloth napkin, all the while holding
on tensely to my burrito. With some trepidation, I took my
third bite. As I chewed slowly, I felt my face getting hotter
and hotter by the second. I was so embarrassed by their jeer-
ing; I didn't know what to do. I just kept my gaze on my
napkin and didn't look at any of them.

Scanning the room as discreetly as I could, I saw Nene who was sitting three tables away with her friends. Without saying a word, I picked up my burrito, my lunch pail, and my cloth napkin, got up, and walked over to my older sister.

She saw me coming up with my burrito in hand, and the tears were streaming down my face, leaving streaks on my face. She moved over to make room for me, and she and all her girlfriends asked me what had happened. Nene's friend, Rosie, gave me her napkin and told me to blow my runny nose, wipe my face off, and sit down with them.

I took a deep breath, wiped off my face, blew my nose, and then told them about the kids laughing at my lunch. My sister turned the reddest I'd ever seen her turn. She told me to point them out to her, and I did. She and Rosie got up and started to walk over to the first grader's table. Annie leaned over and told Vicky and Brady something, and they looked over to my sister and Rosie who were headed their way. They grabbed what was left of their lunches and ran out of the cafeteria.

Confrontation averted, Nene and Rosie turned right around and sat back down.

I finally unloaded the burden I'd been carrying all week. I told my sister what Brady had said earlier in the week about being like chocolate milk and not white milk. I didn't know why my friends were acting differently. My sister told me she'd had a similar experience the year before and that was why she still preferred to go home for lunch. But this year, even though she still would rather eat at home, she didn't mind bringing a lunch because all her friends brought food from home just like hers, and if they didn't, they always wanted to share their food so everyone got to sample a variety of food.

She told me that some kids like to pick on anyone or anything that is different or that they don't understand. And

I said, "You mean like the boys picking on Brady because he is chubby?"

"Yeah, just like that," she said. "But sometimes it can be about things like the food you eat or the language your family speaks at home or how poor your family is or maybe even," she paused, "like the color of your skin or your last name. It's all the same, really. Some people just feel more important if they make someone else feel small. So you shouldn't ever pay attention to people that are mean like that. Okay?"

Wow, and just like that, the dark cloud that had been hanging over my head evaporated, and I said, "Okay, Nene. I'll try."

The following week, I asked my mom to make me another lunch just like she'd made the previous week. I went to the cafeteria and sat down with Annie, Vicky, and Brady. What broke the ice with my friends that day were the two burritos I brought. A whole one for me and one cut into thirds. I gave a piece to Brady, Annie, and Vicky so they could see what a great cook my mom was.

After their simple apologies for acting like idiots, they bit into their sample lunches. They were surprised the food tasted so good and wondered if my mom could teach their moms to make the same kind of lunch for them too. They confessed that they hated the sandwiches their moms made for them and wished their moms could cook like mine.

I ended up feeling pretty special about everything. I finally had decided that being different was a good thing. Even my little Buster Brown haircut had grown out a bit into a cute bob, and pretty soon the other little girls in my class started showing up in school with similar haircuts. And as time passed and I'd gotten over the milk incident, I learned to love chocolate milk and anything chocolate for that matter.

The difficult experiences during my first year in grade school reflect a much simpler time, of course, when our world was not so complicated and children remained children a lot longer. The casualties were more about losing a bit of innocence, the kind of innocence that young children have when there is no difference between race, culture, or religion. When kids are free to just be kids.

Then things mysteriously begin to change, and a child's life hardens. Things are no longer as simple and clear as they once were . . . that being the biggest casualty of all.

And I eventually learned not to worry about any of it.

As my mom had always said . . . it's never the end of the world.

And I knew I would never run out of tears.

Through the Veil

It was late 1978 when we learned that my dad had leukemia and it was terminal.

When he had suddenly begun to feel extreme exhaustion and weakness, which was totally out of character for him, he had gone to see a doctor. He was diagnosed with leukemia. Of course we all thought the small-town doctor had made a terrible mistake and that there was no way in the world Papi could have leukemia. It had to be a mistake.

We insisted he get a second opinion. My mom and dad went to Houston, where all the large medical centers were. My sisters took my dad to Houston Methodist Hospital to be examined by a top oncologist who came highly recommended and specialized in cancer of the blood. The earlier diagnosis my dad had been given was confirmed by the oncologist. The doctor told us the leukemia was in an advanced stage and it was unlikely my dad would live for more than one or two months. Papi lived for almost a year after the diagnosis.

My sisters, Ana and Nene, lived in Houston, so they were able to care for both my mom and dad while he went through all the testing and treatments, which kept them in Houston for several months. My sisters made sure that everything that could be done for my dad was done. They were heroic in their efforts.

Over the course of that last year, he also had a stroke that was directly related to his leukemia, and he recovered within a month, although the doctors had predicted he would never recover from the stroke.

However, the time finally came when his condition continued to deteriorate and the doctors told him there was little or nothing else they could do for him, so they suggested he return home, try to get as comfortable as possible, and do the things he wanted to do. As his leukemia worsened, he became a frequent visitor to the hospital for blood transfusions. And that was only a Band-Aid of sorts, never meant to cure him but only extend his time on earth.

Papi had always been very healthy with a robust constitution. I can't remember a time when he was ever sick or bedridden. There might have been one time when he had a bit of a cold but that's about it. He was also a proud and fiercely independent man. Papi never asked for help from anyone and always took pride in his strength and fortitude.

For him to suddenly become dependent on someone else, even his wife, to help him in and out of bed or to help him with bathing or dressing was a great humiliation. He had never been helpless before. And once his illness became more severe, he was bedridden. This frustrated him and at times angered him because he no longer had control over his body. He did his best to accept the help that was offered, but it was obvious he struggled with his helplessness.

But this last memory is perhaps the deepest, most significant, and most profound memory I have of my father.

It is embedded with sadness, loss, grief, tears, gratitude, and wonder as I remember that night.

This memory is about death and dying, about the thin veil that separates the world of the living and of those who have moved on. Of the inter-connectedness of the two worlds and of the bonds of love that remain strong against all odds.

Death . . . it's a subject most people avoid talking about, avoid thinking about, avoid being near, avoid reading about, and avoid understanding.

I don't know that much about death either. But over the last forty years, I've read about it in spiritual, religious, philosophical, and literary writings by many pundits, gurus, ascetics, teachers, monks, philosophers, poets, and average writers.

None of those writings and teachings have ever given me a real understanding or experience of what death means, what it feels like, and where your soul goes. In spiritual scriptures, we're told we are not the body; we are the spirit, consciousness, awareness, spark, or soul that lies within the physical form. But without a concrete, experiential, and personal experience, these are just words.

My dad's condition became more critical, and in late September, he was admitted into the hospital. Days passed, and he was not getting better, which was expected in this late stage of his cancer.

On one of those last nights, I had gone to the hospital to stay by his side. The doctors had prepared us for the worst. We knew he didn't have much time left, and we just wanted to be with him as much as possible. Of course, he was mostly unconscious. At times, he slipped in and out, would open his eyes, mumble a few words, and then be gone again. Later in the evening, he began to toss and turn and utter a few words incoherently. I felt the energy in the room begin to change. It seemed obvious to me that he was having some sort of internal conflict. And at times, he looked as though he was having a battle with forces outside his own self. It actually frightened me. I was at a loss to fully understand what I was witnessing, and I didn't know what I could do to help. I began chanting Sanskrit mantras and chants that I knew, hoping it would help him in some way. After some time, the struggle ended, and my dad calmed down. I sensed another palpable shift of energy in the room.

Perhaps Papi had made peace with his life, his past, his regrets, his fears, or his unrequited dreams. Who can say? However, a softness came over his face, and everything was light and had an aura of brightness, clarity, and for lack of a better word, cleanliness, as though whatever had upset him had been completely washed away and no longer existed.

I was certain that what I'd witnessed was something out of the corporeal world. It showed me that my dad was beginning to pass through the thin veils of separation between our world and the astral or heavenly realms.

It was getting very late, and my dad still remained unaware of his surroundings. We had decided that my mom would come in to take the night shift with my dad, and I would go back home to get some rest.

While my mom was standing outside in the hallway talking with the night shift doctor, I leaned in to give my dad a kiss goodnight.

He suddenly opened his eyes as though he had just been taking a short nap. Papi had a completely lucid look on his face, and his eyes were sharp and aware. He said good night to me and told me that he loved me. I gave his fragile body a gentle hug so as not to cause any more bruising on his leukemia-ravaged body and kissed him goodnight. I told him I loved him too.

And just then, he told me clearly and in a tone of conversation that sounded as though nothing at all was wrong with him, "*Tengas mucho cuidado manejando cuando te regreses a la casa. Hay una neblina muy gruesa y peligrosa afuera y va ser muy difícil para ver cuando estés manejando. Vete muy despacito. Tengas mucho cuidado.*" (Be very careful driving home. There is a very thick and dangerous fog outside, and it is going to be very difficult for you to see while you are driving. Go very slowly. Be very careful.) And then he closed his eyes, and the room was silent.

I thought that was pretty weird. He hadn't spoken all day, and then all of a sudden, he gave me a weather report?

I said goodnight to my mom and walked out of the hospital. As I headed out to my car in the parking lot, I noticed that it was pretty dreary weather. I pulled out of the hospital parking lot and made a left turn onto the long stretch of country road when I realized I couldn't see anything, even with headlights. There was a dark and thick fog, the likes of which I'd never seen before. The driving visibility was close to zero, making me question my ability to drive home safely. It was exactly as my dad had told me it would be.

As the connection of what he had just told me and what I was actually experiencing began to set in, I felt my body suddenly chill and then become so cold that I began to shiver. I think I was feeling shock more than anything else. How could my dad have possibly known about the fog unless he was already mostly out of his body? It became obvious to me that he was going back and forth across those veils that separate our worlds and that soon he would go through the final veil and wouldn't be returning.

Papi felt so much love and concern for me, even as he lay there dying, that he had forced his consciousness back into this world to warn me about the dangerous road conditions outside.

Nothing I had read in any books or heard in any spiritual

discourses had ever shown me what the moment of death might be like.

My father once again left me stunned with a powerful life lesson. On that fog-drenched night in September, he gave me a glimpse of death . . . an experience of the transition between worlds. He showed me that we are just one thin veil apart from each other. That we are as close to each other as whispers or sighs. That the veils are so thin they can move with every breath or shift in energy. That there is little that separates these worlds and it is the consciousness in our physical bodies that keeps those veils solid and immobile. Once we come out of our bodies and allow our consciousness to expand, we begin to feel those veils flutter.

And even more amazing to me was my father's concern for my wellbeing. How could he ever have had the strength to come back to me to tell me, one last time, that he loved me and to be aware of my safety, as he had done on so many other occasions in my life?

How would I ever be able to repay his love? Would I ever be able to tell him enough times that I loved him too and that I wished him well on his next journey and that I wished him only blessings?

The next day, I was at the hospital again. I sat by his side all that afternoon and evening, holding his hand and chanting softly, hoping to sooth his heart. After several hours of silence, he let out a deep breath, almost like a sigh of relief. I thought he was still alive. Then the nurse walked in. My dad let out one more breath. The nurse came around the bed to my side and, with tears in his eyes, told me my father was gone. That had been his last breath. I didn't want to believe it. How could it be? He had just been breathing, and that was a deep breath I had seen. I had no idea what a last breath was at the time, but now I do.

My dad was gone.

I had done nothing special in my life to make me deserve to be with my dad at that moment. But whether or not I deserved the honor, I was given it nonetheless. I sent him all the loving thoughts I could gather in that moment and bundled them up and placed them in his heart. I asked the universe to take as good care of his soul as he had taken care of us all our lives. To watch over him, protect him, and nurture him as he'd done for us all those years. And to fill him with love, light, and happiness.

Papi died on September 28, 1979, at the relatively young age of seventy-one. We still miss him and wish we could have had him with us longer. We know he would have loved knowing about all the latest advances in science and technology, the cable stations and satellite television, internet, cell phones, GPS, laptop computers, Kindle and iPods . . .

I console myself knowing that he is just where he needs to be and that we are never far apart. That all loving hearts are forever connected in this universe and that love is never gone; it continues to evolve and grow.

My father was a great teacher of mine, and he continues to teach me as I delve deeply into my past and remember his love.

To my father, I give thanks.

La Música

TUNCHE, TUNCHE, TUNCHE. When I heard the familiar rhythm, an iconic tunche, tunche, tunche beat
resounding from across the road, I knew it had to be either
Tuesday or Thursday night in Captain Cook, Hawaii, where
my husband and I were living at the time.

The lively music of this dedicated band pulsated from the
covered deck of the blue house. A wave of notes drifted along
the gentle upcountry breeze directly into our home. The
group of musicians gathered twice a week to practice. They
would play for hours, and it was always the same traditional
Mexican ranch-style music. When I was young, my parents
told me this style of music was called *música ranchera*. It was
inspired by life out on the ranches of Mexico, of a simple
life far from large urban centers. Over time, música ranchera
became popular and mainstream in Mexico, as well as across
the border in the United States.

I simply refer to it as "tunche" music. This was exactly
how I heard and processed the underlying beat. I loved it as a
child and quite possibly love it more even now that I'm older.

After all those months, I never did find out the name of the band that gathered on those nights years ago. All I knew was they were playing music that resonated with me. I was thrilled their practice sessions went on through several seasons. I'm not sure if they improved over the many months of practice or if they were always that talented. What I do know is that I genuinely enjoyed my private concerts. I was eager for Tuesday and Thursday nights to arrive.

For most practice nights, the music was so loud it sounded as if they were playing in our driveway. On more than one occasion, our neighbor Clarence phoned to ask if the music was bothering us. He complained that he couldn't hear his television program, even with the volume turned all the way up due to the blasting music. I had no complaints about how high the amps were set or how long they played. Though I hungered for more music, the band was respectful and would normally finish practice by 9:00 p.m. My poor neighbor was forced to suffer the throes of loud música ranchera all on his own. On the other hand, I would have been happy had they played all night.

On those evenings, I enjoyed going out to our lanai to listen and dance to the upbeat tunes. I even considered, however briefly, that I could have a small dinner party on a Tuesday or Thursday night. To entice my guests with live music would have been stretching the truth of course but would not have been a complete fabrication. I see now there were multiple missed opportunities for night soirées.

I realize why this particularly loud music didn't bother me. Música ranchera was my soul music. It penetrated deep into my roots, my early childhood memories, and perhaps, even my DNA. Although my parents much preferred classical Mexican singers such as Pedro Infante or Jorge Negrete, they loved all forms of Mexican music, including música ranchera and the exuberant mariachi bands.

When I was young, anytime I wanted to listen to soothing music, I could choose from the extensive classical album collection my father had curated. There was everything from Beethoven to Mozart and all the greats in between. However, I don't recall there being any albums of humble ranch music.

When I was growing up in the Texas border town of Brownsville, the opportunity to hear Mexican music was not out of the ordinary. Since 1938, the town has honored its connection and friendship to its sister city across the border, Matamoros, Mexico, with a yearly festival, Charro Days. The week is filled with Mexican music, parades, floats, food, and school children dancing traditional regional Mexican dances in authentic attire. This event continues to be celebrated to this day. And música ranchera remains a familiar sound of Charro Days.

Every summer, we visited my grandmother and aunt in Mexico. The weather was usually sweltering hot that time of year. It forced us all to sleep outside at night in the back courtyard on army cots. Some of the earliest memories I have of listening to música ranchera were on those nights, sleeping under the stars with the neighborhood cantina right around the corner from my grandmother's house. The music was loud and went on late into the night. The songs mingled with loud shouting from inebriated customers. Eventually, the music would drown out the noise and lull me to sleep.

It was common, during my college years, to go out drinking with friends. Living in a border town gave us easy access to alcohol, and we would cross into Matamoros on a whim. The fact that bars never checked to see if you were of legal drinking age was a big draw for clandestine day drinking trips for some high school and college kids. Besides limitless access to cheap alcohol, the nice cocktail bars and the oh-so shady cantinas had one element that remained a given, and that was the music. My tunche, tunche, tunche music.

That I am a lover of music is an understatement. I give credit to my parents for bringing music into our home and into my life at a young age. The beat of ranch music remains ingrained in my memory and in my heart. It makes me happy, and it soothes my spirit.

I lived in Hawaii over forty years. During those years I learned that Hawaiian music is steeped in history and permeates local culture. Most Hawaiians probably have someone in their family that can either play musical instruments, sing, or dance hula. They are often musically gifted, and music, being a valued tradition, is nurtured and handed down through generations.

The local families in our Captain Cook neighborhood would have boisterous get-togethers. Pop-up canopies were set up in front and back yards days ahead of an event. *Ohana*, family and friends, would arrive a day ahead of the celebration and often stayed for a few days afterwards. There was always singing and music and most definitely there would be an auntie or two performing hula.

Generational memories and cultural traditions were created during the music-filled gatherings. They remain long after an individual is gone. Music, dance, and song are all vital forces in our lives that deserve a place of honor.

Now that I live in the Pacific Northwest, I have had the opportunity to attend various totem pole blessing ceremonies. There, I have experienced the music, drumming, and chanting of the indigenous Coast Salish people. I recognize it as an integral part of their life and culture, of their history, and of the story still being told.

On those Tuesday and Thursday evenings so many years ago in our Hawaiian home, as I listened to the songs played by the musicians, I recognized that they carried a spark into my life that rekindled the memories from my childhood and youth, of my connectedness to my family, culture, and heritage. Música ranchera did all that for me and more.

Music can be unending inspiration and fuel for creativity. The vibration that emerges carries its own claim to fame. It can be a gentle teacher; it can be a great healer. At its best, music can uplift spirits, broaden horizons, and transcend cultural differences.

Strolling Backwards,
a Conclusion

I'VE SHARED WITH YOU A TAPESTRY of stories about my childhood and other times of my life. Some of these stories were intertwined with descriptions of the food and aromas that were key ingredients to my childhood memories. They were painted with the lively and vibrant colors of my cultural experiences and heritage. Interwoven throughout the stories were the lessons learned along the way.

Hopefully you came to the same conclusion that I came to—that we aren't so different from each other after all. Though our cultures, traditions, foods, and upbringing may have been different, we share similar stories and memories that transcend cultural differences. Though we may walk in different shoes, in the end, we all have walking in common.

Acknowledgments

To Richard, my husband, *mahalo nui loa*, thank you very much, for being supportive every step of the way.

I thank my sisters, Ana and Irene, who believe I can accomplish even my wildest dreams.

I am grateful to my three precious border collies who always brightened my days and nights.

My generous friends, Coral Mack (Hawaii/Oregon) and Cathe Howe (Mill Valley, California), I thank for lending their eyes to proofing and editing in the early stages.

With humility, I thank my extraordinary friend, Margarita Rosenthal (Millbrae, California) who, during the final months of her life as she battled cancer, found time out of the precious "good days" to do a final edit of my book. Her selfless spirit graces each story, page, and line of this book. Mahalo, Margarita.

I thank Village Book Publishing, from the beginning all the way to the end, for the staff going above and beyond to get my book out again into the world. Special thanks to Chloe Hovind, Stephanie Dethlefs, and Jessica Moreland.

Melissa Vail Coffman of Book House Publishing, thank

you for the layout and beautiful design work for *Border Town Chica*.

To Book House Publishing and Bob Paltrow Design for working collaboratively and harmoniously on the book cover design.

To Julie Scandora, editor, thank you for working so diligently on my book.

Patricia Alarcón Missler was born in Brownsville, a sleepy South Texas border town. She is a first generation Mexican American. Patricia was the youngest of five children, growing up in a modest neighborhood. Her earlier influences were her parents and her extended family. Her parents were artistically inclined and passed on their appreciation of beauty to Patricia. They instilled in her a deep respect for her roots. Patricia saw Mexico and its beautiful culture firsthand, at a very young age, travelling throughout many parts of Mexico with her parents and visiting her beloved grandmother and aunt in Nuevo Laredo on summer vacations. This cultural immersion enhanced her love of Mexican art, architecture, vibrant colors, and exotic foods. Patricia graduated from the University of Texas at Austin with a major in sociology and a minor in English. While living in Texas, she worked as a social worker for many years.

Upon moving to Hawaii, Patricia had an artistic awakening. She discovered and embraced her natural artistic inclinations by taking the opportunity to study with many well-known artists and has herself become a successful painter. She and her husband are both painters and writers. Together they created, curated, and operated their own art gallery in Hawaii for sixteen years. They also designed and built a home tucked away in a native Hawaiian forest, further expressing their creative energy.

Patricia shares that "Writing has always been an essential element in my life. My experience in painting helps create colorful images with my words. Writing is a natural and organic partner to my painting."

Visit the author's websites:
www.patriciamissler.com
www.bordertownchica.com

Printed in the USA
CPSIA information can be obtained
at www.ICGtesting.com
CBHW060716240624
10279CB00012B/19